Shaihu Umar

African Creative Writing Series

General Editor: Michael J. C. Echeruo
Professor of English,
University of Ibadan

Shaihu Umar

Umaru Ladan and Dexter Lyndersay

a play adapted from the novel by
Sir Abubakar Tafawa Balewa

Longman

Longman Group Limited London

Associated companies, branches and
representatives throughout the world

First Published 1975
Reprinted 1987, 1989
ISBN 0582 64192 6

Printed in Nigeria by
The Caxton Press (West Africa) Limited, Ibadan

Authors' Note

The novel *Shaihu Umar*, by the late Alhaji Sir Abubakar Tafawa Balewa, contains the essence of Hausa and Islamic culture and is a beautifully compact tale of Shaihu Umar's adventures as child and man.

In our adaptation to the difficult medium of a stage presentation, certain liberties have been taken with the plot and cast of characters which serve to carry the play along dramatically and also to provide specific and general information which were not necessary in the novel.

New characters include Kwatau, the Rauhani (invisible to those on stage) and the Wawan Sarki. Other characters from the novel may have more or different tasks, better or worse tempers. We expect that further changes may be necessary when a film version of *Shaihu Umar* is produced.

Our purpose was to stage a play, and yet be as faithful to the novel as possible. Our hope is that you will be entertained.

Umaru Ladan
Dexter Lyndersay

The Setting

The setting is a large bare raised rectangular area bounded on three sides by a measure of equally bare stage. In the middle of the fourth side, at the back, there is an adjoining alcove covered by a circular roof. Access to the roof from the rectangular area is by two crescent-shaped stairs on either side. The interior of the alcove is one step up from the main area and there is also an entrance to it from the back of the stage, covered with a cloth.

Acknowledgements

The publishers acknowledge the Northern Nigerian Publishing Company as holders of the copyright of the original Hausa novel by Sir Abubakar Tafawa Balewa, and Mervyn Hiskett as translator of the English version of the novel published by Longman in 1967.

The photographs between pages 4 and 5 and 20 and 21 were taken by Dexter Lyndersay.

The authors are grateful to John E. Lavers for the opening dialogue of the scholars.

Foreword

Since its official inauguration on 1 July 1972 the Centre for Nigerian Cultural Studies has enjoyed rapid and considerable success. Within three months it was able to recruit well-trained, experienced and relevant staff in the four cultural areas of music, drama, dance and archaeology. In addition, it was able to recruit Nigerian counterparts with tremendous potential. The Centre was thus encouraged to accept the challenge of a major dramatic production in Hausa for the tenth anniversary celebrations of Ahmadu Bello University. For this important first presentation the choice fell upon *Shaihu Umar*, a play adapted by Umaru Ladan and Dexter Lyndersay from the novel by the late first Prime Minister of the Nigerian Federation, Sir Abubakar Tafawa Balewa, M.H.R.

The play was performed on various occasions to various appreciative audiences with such success that it is not only being published in Hausa by the Northern Nigerian Publishing Company and in this English version by Longman, but it is also being filmed. The Federal Film Unit, in co-operation with the Centre for Nigerian Cultural Studies, is making a full-length feature film of *Shaihu Umar* as Nigeria's film entry in the second World Black Arts Festival of Arts and Culture, thus bringing the play to a much wider audience.

We at Ahmadu Bello University are proud to be associated not only with the production of the play but also with the publication of both the Hausa and English versions. We can think of no better way to honour the memory of the first Prime Minister of our great country.

I. S. Audu,
Vice-Chancellor,
Ahmadu Bello University

The Scenes

ACT I

Scene 1 Morning Prayer; the market; the scholars; Shaihu Umar
Scene 2 The funeral; the birth; the Rauhani
Scene 3 Fatimah's compound
Scene 4 The marriage ceremony
Scene 5 The Chief's court; the pagan ritual; the night raid; the Chief's court
Scene 6 Makau's compound
Scene 7 Makau's journey; the hunter; the travellers
Scene 8 The Chief's court (three years later); Fatimah's compound
Scene 9 The kidnapping; the hyena; the rescue; the second kidnapping
Scene 10 Fatika: outside Fatimah's family's compound

ACT II

Scene 1 Kano: Gumuzu's compound
Scene 2 The Sahara; the oasis
Scene 3 Ber Kufa: learning the Koran; the Muharram feast
Scene 4 **Dream:** the kidnapping of the lioness's cub; the hunters' camp; the fork in the road; the Arab camp
Reality: Makarfi; Kano; Murzuk; Tripoli
Scene 5 Ber Kufa: Abdulkarim's house
Scene 6 Tripoli: Ahmad's house
Scene 7 The sandstorm
Scene 8 Kwatau's court; the pagan farm raid; Kwatau's court; the prayer

The Cast

The names of the actors given here are those who appeared in the first performance. The play was first produced by the Centre for Nigerian Cultural Studies, Ahmadu Bello University, in association with the Maitama Sule Dramatic Group and student actors of Abdullahi Bayero College ABU Kano Campus, and performed in Hausa at Government Lodge, Kaduna, on 1 December 1972 for His Excellency the former Head of State, General Yakubu Gowon, and Mrs Gowon, on the occasion of His Excellency's assumption of the office of Visitor of Ahmadu Bello University during its tenth anniversary celebrations.

SHAIHU UMAR	Umaru Ladan
BEGGAR (Maroki)	Audu Muhammadu Ashana
IMAM OF KAGARA (present)	Dandu Ahmed
SENIOR SCHOLAR 1	Shehu Ladan
SENIOR SCHOLAR 2	Abdussalam Abdallah
IMAM OF KAGARA (past)	Umaru Uba Gaya
FATIMAH (Umar's mother)	Fatima Balla
MOTHER-IN-LAW (Umar's father's mother)	Bilkisu Uwani Ibrahim
AMINA (Fatimah's friend)	Zainab Dasuki
RAUHANI (Umar's invisible protector)	Peter Badejo
UMAR (aged 2)	Abubakar S. Abubakar
MAKAU (Fatimah's second husband)	Dasuki Sulaimanu
SINGER (Mawaki)	A. M. Ashana
CHIEF OF KAGARA	Abdulmumuni Chiranchi
WAWAN SARKI (the Court Fool)	Haruna Kumbul
KWATAU (the Chief's younger brother)	Mansur Kwalli
SARKIN ZAGI (protector of the Chief)	Rufa'i Omar Madaki
SHANTALI (Kwatau's kinsman)	Mustapha Mohammed
BUHARI (Amina's husband)	Dahiru Hudu

ANGRY PAGAN MAN	Namadi Abdullahi
UMAR (aged 6 to 9 years)	Ibrahim Lavers
HUNTER	Sarki Aliyu
TRAVELLER 1	Shu'aibu Adamu Biu
TRAVELLER 2	Idi Zurmi
ISA (Makau's messenger)	A. M. Ashana
JAKADIYA (female messenger)	Zainab Budun
HYENA	Mohammed Yusufu
UMAR'S FOSTER-MOTHER	Talatu Halilu
UMAR'S FOSTER-FATHER	Dan Yaro Mariri
GUMUZU (Kano slave-trader)	Munzali Jibril
BA'IMANI (Gumuzu's henchman)	Aliyu Bala Umar
NEWS CARRIER	A. M. Ashana
ABDULKARIM (Arab slave-trader)	Othman Abdulkadir Jilani
ARAB MERCHANT	Bashir Abubakar
UMAR (as a scholar)	Kabiru Mohammed
SHEIKH MAS'UD (Imam of Ber Kufa)	Sani Abdullahi Tofa
LIONESS (Dream)	Amina Ladan
CUB (Dream)	Ibrahim Lavers
ADO (Kano slave trader)	Ibrahim Mohammed
CADI (Judge in Murzuk)	Umaru Uba Gaya
AHMAD (Tripoli slave-trader)	Akibu Aminu
EXECUTIONER (in Kwatau's court)	Bako Kaduna
BODYGUARD (to Chief of Kagara)	Mijinyawa Bello

Junior scholars; wedding guests; court warriors; citizens; Arabs; pagans; raiders; entertainers; hunters; children; searchers; slaves; slave guards; Makau's household; book-carrier; Cadi's herald; musicians; caravaneers; farmers

Voices: Ladan (muezzin)
Kewa (funeral sympathy)
Koran (teacher)

Production Notes

Introduction

If any reader wants to produce *Shaihu Umar*, these notes offer opportunities to discover those areas in which the potential director/designer might be strong and those which might need expert help. There are also useful guidelines designed to avoid pitfalls which the first directors found by trial and error.

Of course, the directors do not believe that the first was the only or best way. But so many facets of the first presentation could not be conveyed in the stage directions but contributed so much to its success, that I thought they should be put on record for the sake of those interested—whether theatre practitioners or theatregoers.

Here then are some of the problems of detail which faced the production team of this new play set, at the turn of the present century, mainly in Hausaland, Nigeria.

Casting

This is the kind of play which is welcomed by those in charge of large numbers of people—usually students—who are interested in drama and who would each be glad of even a small part in a major production.

The first cast—a mixture of students and semi-professional performers—numbered ninety-two with some doubling and tripling of parts. A hundred and twenty or more could be used if necessary.

However, many producers find such large casts a burden and would prefer possibilities to multiply the number of roles each performer can take. By adopting the following suggestions, the cast could be limited to about fifty-five.

Fifteen parts should be played by one performer throughout. They are:

SHAIHU UMAR, the storyteller

UMAR, the scholar, aged 30

UMAR, aged 2 (but his appearance is not essential)
SENIOR SCHOLAR 1
SENIOR SCHOLAR 2
FATIMAH, Umar's mother
RAUHANI, the Compassion of Allah
WAWAN SARKI, the Court Fool
KWATAU, brother to the Chief of Kagara
SHANTALI, Kwatau's kinsman
and The KUKUMA Player (see Music)
The GOGE Player (see Music)
3 MUSICIANS (see Music)

Nearly all the others can play multiple roles. For instance, the same actor can play UMAR, aged 6 to 9, and the LION CUB; another actor can double the roles of MAKAU and the HYENA; the same actress can play the MOTHER-IN-LAW and the LIONESS and another actress can play the JAKADIYA and the FOSTER MOTHER. The crowd players obviously take as many parts as possible. The same costumes can be used for the MARKETEERS, NEIGHBOURS and CITIZENS; for the boys and girls in their different scenes as MARKET CHILDREN, Umar's PLAYMATES, URCHINS and CHILDREN of CITIZENS, while the two groups of ARABS must be distinguished from each other by their costumes.

Design of the setting

The set design for the first production was as described in the text. (*Note that the photographs do not show the 16′ × 20′ (4·8m × 6m) platform stage 2′–6″ (75cm) high, only the rear alcove area and steps on the flat ground.*) The audience sat on three sides of the playing area.

The playing areas

The top of the alcove was reserved for SHAIHU UMAR the story-teller, and the two SENIOR SCHOLARS. Alternatively, the narrating place can be to one side. The crescent-shaped steps, from the top of the alcove to the platform stage, cross over two entrance-ways so that all who pass under them have to bend to do so. Though architecturally impertinent (no doorways are actually shaped like that), the low height is consonant with the Hausa/Muslim practice of forcing humility (the bent-over position) upon those who enter indoors or depart into the world outside.

The crescent in the design is the symbol of the moon which is important in the Muslim religion and can be found, symbolised in countless ways, in religious or fertility ceremonies and artefacts throughout Africa, the Middle East and elsewhere.

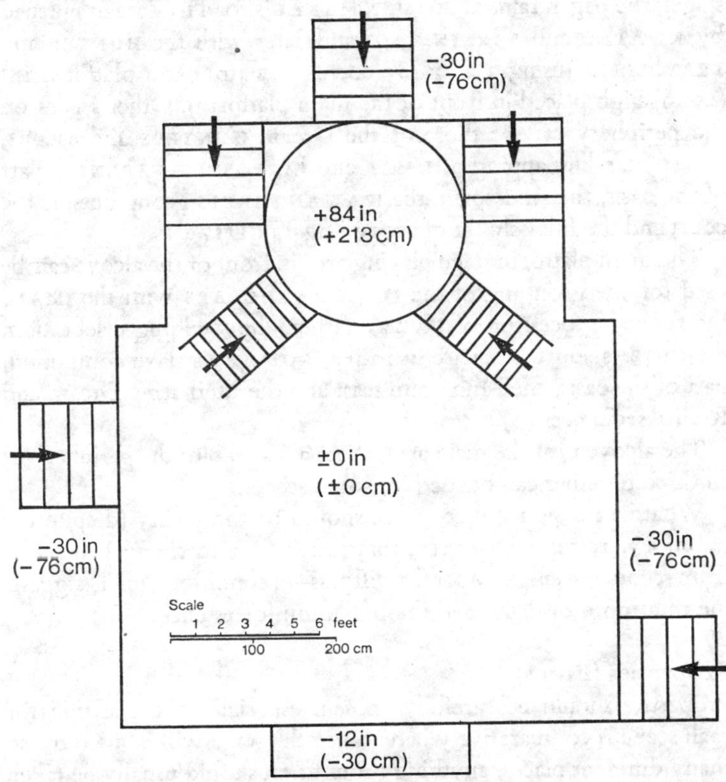

The alcove itself can represent FATIMAH's house, the court canopy for the CHIEF OF KAGARA, the home of BUHARI and AMINA, the HYENA cave, SHEIKH MAS'UD's teaching place, the Dream LIONNESS's cave, MAKAU's home in Makarfi, the CADI's court in Murzuk, ABDULKARIM's home in Ber Kufa, AHMAD's house in Tripoli. In the case of dwelling places for the play's characters, a hanging doorway cloth at the rear of the alcove can be sufficient to suggest the space beyond. A flight of steps leads down past the cloth from the platform stage to the lowest playing level of the periphery. Other step units are placed upstage right and downstage left of the platform.

The periphery can be used for the road to the market in the opening scene (with the BEGGAR to and fro on the edge of the platform stage), the pagan raids at one side, MAKAU's road to Zazzau pursued by KWATAU and SARKIN ZAGI and later with the HUNTER and TRAVELLERS (using a 2′ × 8′ (60cm × 2·4m) extra platform 18″ (45cm) high placed in front of the main platform). Other scenes on the periphery can be those of the Dream HUNTERS and ARABS, GUMUZU's kidnapping of UMAR and his FOSTER-PARENTS, part of the oasis, the sandstorm, the WAWAN SARKI's group outside the court and the final cluster of angry Kagara CITIZENS.

The main platform stage playing area in front of the alcove can be used for the grouping of the JUNIOR SCHOLARS with the IMAM, the funeral procession of UMAR's father, the wedding celebration, the CHIEF's court, a square in Fatika, GUMUZU's slave compound, part of the oasis, the Muharram feast and the alternating Dream and Reality sequences.

The alcove plus the main area, the main area plus the periphery or all three together can be used for some scenes.

Whatever design is used, there should be the ability (despite the use of a narrator which gives that much time to change) to move from scene to scene with some swiftness—a condition which suggests the minimum of detail and the maximum of essence.

Properties (Props)

Properties should be carefully chosen, especially if the setting for each scene is comparatively bare. Since the stage will be used for so many different places, anything brought on should usually be taken off again at the end of each scene or part of a scene.

The opening market scene could include food (in containers or open trays), cooking and storage utensils, artefacts, pottery, clothing on hangers, cloth in bales, grain in bags, cut wood, grass ropes, etc., carried across the front by the marketeers.

For the funeral procession of UMAR's father, four men carry the bier, called *makara* (not buried with the corpse), a 6′ (1·8m) long, 18″ (45cm) wide and 18″ (45cm) deep, rectangular, open-top container made of the spines of palm fronds cut and lashed together with the two edge poles longer by about a foot each for being carried on the shoulders. This is quite heavy and a dummy can be used for the sheet-covered body inside. Incidentally, there are no women in the procession.

Hand cotton-spinning materials include a basket of raw cotton, a roller to facilitate the removal of seeds laid on a large flat stone, a stick fitted to a clay cone from which, in a vertical position, to spin the cotton thread. Mats, brought in and taken off by FATIMAH and the MOTHER-IN-LAW, can be used for the spinning scene.

The junior scholars' slates are of this shape and approximately 24″ (60cm) long by 12″ (30cm) wide.

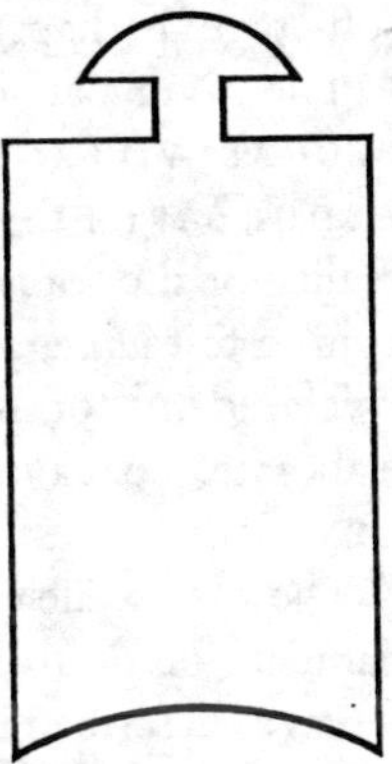

Warriors' swords should be in sheaths connected to bandoliers about the upper body (part of costume). Mats can be used in the court scenes for the seated courtiers but, if setting and removing is a problem, they can be omitted in favour of a good pre-show cleaning of the main platform area to protect the costumes.

Real cloth-wrapped oil-soaked torches (or, for fire control, faked ones using electricity) are needed for the first pagan night raid. If real fire is used, there should be buckets of water offstage to extinguish them afterwards.

Tie-ropes, of woven grass preferably, are needed for the captured PAGANS in the court scene following the raid.

The HUNTER near Zazzau has a gourd of water (real) to offer MAKAU. The travellers on the same road have a blanket and food (real) in leather bags.

Gifts from MAKAU to the CHIEF OF KAGARA through the messenger, ISA, are as described in the text.

SARKIN ZAGI uses a bag of meat and sweets to entice young UMAR away from his playmates. He also has a large, gleaming (dulled-edge) knife to press against UMAR's throat in the cave.

The slave-guards in GUMUZU's compound have whips. The Dream HUNTERS carry bows and arrows. One Dream ARAB has a pistol of European manufacture of the period. A starter's pistol (perhaps disguised) firing blanks or a loud-report cap pistol should be suitable.

Bags of money are exchanged as follows: ADO to GUMUZU; CADI of Murzuk to his HERALD and thence to ADO; AHMAD to HERALD (off-stage, perhaps); HERALD to CADI; ABDULKARIM to AHMAD.

The giving of single coins can be mimed—MARKETEERS to the BEGGAR; VILLAGERS to the NEWS-CARRIER of Fatika; in the oasis; ABDULKARIM to the praise-singers. But coins can be used for the reality of the sound of them together or added business of biting a coin to test its legality.

The CADI of Murzuk can use a large leather cushion or an elaborate, concave-seated stool, brought in and taken off by the HERALD.

The oasis scene of vendors can feature the goods carried in camel-panniers or double 'donkey bags' made of woven grass held by slaves as described in the text. Articles being sold would include raw cotton, artefacts, leather goods, ostrich feathers, rawhide, kolanuts or stage representations of such things.

The Muharram feast requires a large carpet laid out (by attendants) before the Arab participants enter. They drink tea later from small transparent glasses and eat dates off silver trays. Three or four books are brought in by a servant of SHEIKH MAS'UD.

FATIMAH is brought out in chains (real, but light in weight) from AHMAD's house, both for the simultaneous scene with the LIONESS and later when brought out to ABDULKARIM and UMAR.

The PAGAN FARMERS during KWATAU's daylight raid are equipped with short-handled hoes which they later use as weapons. UMAR's FOSTER-FATHER (farming before GUMUZU's entrance) also uses a hoe.

Lighting

The lighting, as with most plays, can be as simple or as complicated as the available equipment allows. It would be well, however, to have separate lighting arrangements for the top of the alcove where the story is being told since there should be a back-and-forth movement of illumination between the action itself and the narrator of it, except when it is desirable (in the Dream) to have both areas lit.

General lighting for the main playing area can be of the warm-on-one-side-cool-on-the-other system with a few variations for the different scenes. For instance, within the alcove itself and just in front of it might be separately lit from the rest because of smaller scenes which happen there.

While the general lighting should include the lower periphery, more specific lighting could be mounted for scenes such as the pagan raids. A follow-spot, or a light which can be moved around with the action, would be useful in such scenes as the progress of MAKAU towards Zazzau and the movement of the LIONESS in the Dream. Indeed the Dream should be differently lit from the Reality alternating with it. A movable light can give flexibility to the lighting designer in emphasising one area or another—the ARAB MERCHANT can be isolated in his juxtaposed exchange about the Sahara with the narrator; UMAR learning the Koran; etc. In such cases, once the light is moved into position, it would be left throughout the scene.

Any back lighting will be an asset, angled from above. A 'steel blue' filter (cool) is suitable during both day and night scenes for this purpose. For night, it could suggest moonlight; for the daylight, it is not blue enough to upset a generally warm illumination and provides the head-and-shoulders definition for the actors which makes them stand out from the background.

For the sandstorm, a warm light at low intensity with hands (or some leaves) passed frequently across the lens (to the accompaniment of the wind sound effect) can suffice.

Please note that the play is suited to outdoor performance (face-to-face or, preferably, with audience on three sides) and the lighting suggested is basic. With an indoor performance and adequate equipment, many more exciting effects are possible.

Sound

The following can be put on tape for the performance:

The voice of the Ladan (muezzin) for the opening morning prayer and for the two o'clock prayer in Fatika ending Act One.

The opening prayer before the Market scene—offstage (if this is done onstage, the men should stand facing East. If East happens to be upstage, or away from the audience, the men, bowing during the prayer, could present a poor picture).

The voice of the Kewa (funeral sympathy) can be on tape or live.

Wind and thunder to accompany lightning light effects for the FATIMAH/RAUHANI scene.

A newborn baby crying.

A horn and gong for the departure signal of the caravan of ABDULKARIM.

The voice of the Koranic teacher, SHEIKH MAS'UD, can be live or on tape, but UMAR the scholar must be able to repeat the Koranic chapters, reasonably well, himself.

Costumes

The play was still in scenario or synopsis form in English when a copy of it, accompanied by a list of the characters and their relationships to each other, was given to the Costume Designer with his first briet. This was to choose costume styles which could have been in existence during the late nineteenth and early twentieth centuries—the period of the play's events. This meant, in fact, that, for the Hausa dress, there would be no buttons, collars or embroidery on caps, and also that garments would be of the simplest cut.

Depth of research, an aesthetic sense and 'artistic licence' guide directors and designers of a play set in a period which is sparsely documented as to costume. The design procedure for a play where the style and details of dress are already distinctive constitutes artistic choice of existing designs and patterns to make a visual theatrical impact. During the process, the period of the play, the location of each scene, the character and occupation of the wearer are taken into account. Other practical considerations are the objects which may have to be concealed on the performer's person (pockets) and the type of movement expected of the wearer (energetic, majestic, or other).

The selection of colours is both an aesthetic and a psychological exercise. Groups, in a family, a court, a single activity or in a community, when going about their business in real life, might contain individuals who think nothing about relating to others in the group by dress or colour. But, on the stage, it is desirable that the audience be able (especially in large-cast, epic plays) to identify groups—and their rebels. Often this is a subconscious realisation, but usually the subconscious is led to it by the designer.

The court of the CHIEF of Kagara, for instance, was dressed pre dominantly in browns with beiges and mustards and off-white mixtures. The CHIEF himself blended in a moss-green *al-kyabba* (burnous, or hooded cloak) over white, while KWATAU, his younger brother (a 'villain'), dressed in beige, showed a 'more acid' green in his *taguwa* underdress. This shade of green was repeated in the turban of SARKIN ZAGI (another 'villain' but also an important protector of the Chief). The JAKADIYA (female messenger) wore a more positive bottle-green with white and lighter green patterns and MAKAU, the chief warrior, had a *riga* with grass-green embroidery to round out the use of the green in the court.

By their actions in the court and subsequently together, the acidity of the shade of green was justified for KWATAU and SARKIN ZAGI, while the other shades of green for the CHIEF and JAKADIYA made pleasanter statements. Further into the court, the browns were diluted for the bodyguard by white patches in the traditional jigsaw juxtaposition and the warriors donned colourful battle garments. The FOOL was mostly in yellow, extravagantly cut, with black and brown markings.

In choosing light grass-green embroidery for MAKAU's maroon *riga*, one could suggest his grouping (as the CHIEF's favourite) with the ruling family, but his gown's maroon colour placed him with another family grouping: his own. For, also wearing maroon in varying shades, were SHAIHU UMAR (as the storyteller and also at the three other ages mentioned in his narration) as well as his mother, FATIMAH (MAKAU's wife), in all changes of costume. Later on, ABDULKARIM, who was a father to UMAR for most of his student life, would have maroon in one of his costumes.

FATIMAH's MOTHER-IN-LAW and their friend, AMINA, wore different shades of indigo (blue) and two of FATIMAH's costumes, in scenes with these two, contained a measure of indigo with her maroon.

As a general rule, whenever we could stick to it, the colours chosen for Nigerians were those which could have been obtained through the use of vegetable dyes. The CHIEF and his court might show exceptions because wealth would buy the importations through North Africa. But, for the North African characters (Arabs) and in the locations where coloured cloth was already being imported for general use, the colours could be brighter and more varied.

Research into Hausa dress yields valuable information on *wando* (trousers), *taguwa* (a long shirt with sleeves and a circular neck), *riga* (a large, square gown), *jallabia* (an ankle-length gown), men's turbans and women's head-ties. The North African clothes would feature such garments as the *falmaran* (waistcoat), *djellaba* (open-necked robe), *kaftan* (various styles) and *kaffiyeh* (head-dress) according to character. Some Fulani dress—*binjima* (a tunic with a flared skirt)—was introduced for the hunters and searchers near the hyena cave to emphasise the distance which the kidnapper had taken UMAR.

Make-up

SHAIHU UMAR, the IMAM and RAUHANI should have grey beards, but no moustaches.

RAUHANI's hair make-up, including eyebrows, is almost white.

The CHIEF OF KAGARA can have a grey beard (optional), but no moustache.

UMAR, as a scholar and as Sheikh, can have a moustache, but no beard.

MOTHER-IN-LAW might have a few teeth missing, as might the FOOL.

The chief PAGAN RITUAL DANCER, before the night raid, should have blue on his face; the others, optional.

Before Act Two begins, KWATAU, SHANTALI and WAWAN SARKI must be aged.

Before FATIMAH's last entrance, she should be aged and withered considerably.

Masks

Animal masks can be of any degree of ingenuity. The full body of the human performer can be dressed to complete the animal, but a gown or loincloth might be of more artistic use.

Directing

Hausa-speaking audiences for Hausa drama can sit (and sometimes stand) for hours to watch the development of a dramatic piece which is mostly verbal. The Maitama Sule Dramatic Group, named after the current Chairman of the Nigerian Arts Council, has a repertoire of plays which contain a number of visually lively scenes but, in general, plays in Hausa tend to contain long scenes of seated performers in discussion or argument, visually varied by hand gestures, adjustments of position and/or clothing and the occasional entry or exit of characters. This is in the Hausa/Muslim tradition where, for instance, once the Chief has sat down, only privileged persons may stand without permission before he does. People do sit to talk, on mats or cushions in the traditional way, and there is seldom justification (or 'motivation') for getting up again until the conversation is over.

This is how the audience likes it and the reasons for this style to prevail are very strong indeed. In *Shaihu Umar*, there is a quantity of necessary action which makes the still or static scenes work as contrast in the overall pacing of the play. The longest scene (in the CHIEF's court after the first pagan raid when MAKAU is denounced by his jealous rivals) is broken logically by a command for a musical display, the interruption of which (by the entrance of the CHIEF's favourite, MAKAU, with only two slaves instead of the discussed four) can be especially chilling.

In general, reasonable respect should be employed for the teachings of Islam—in references to Allah and the use of the Koran (the JUNIOR SCHOLARS' slates should *not* have real Koranic excerpts written on them, but some substitute Arabic script).

Comments relative to authentic movement of some of the characters, such as the RAUHANI, in the blocking can be found under Movement.

Movement

The following notes are not in order of occurrence in the play.

The FOOL's movements are exaggerated hops from one foot to the other, so that only at rest are both feet on the ground near each other.

Performers' hands during prayer are extended forwards almost parallel to the floor with open palms upward. The closing word 'Amin' brings the hands together, still open, towards the face, fingers to the forehead briefly.

In the first court scene, courtiers are already standing to greet the CHIEF shaking their raised right fists in solidarity. When the CHIEF is seated, they sit on the floor with ankles together and to the left of the thighs. After the first pagan raid, each courtier enters with his bound captive(s), pushes the pagan(s) down in front of the CHIEF, the courtier himself briefly going onto one knee. Then he herds off his captive(s), with the aid of the BODYGUARD, upstage, before returning to his place to sit.

MAKAU enters in this way with his two slaves. Throughout the queries of the CHIEF he remains on one knee. The BODYGUARD pushes the two slaves off at the start of the dialogue. Except for KWATAU, SARKIN ZAGI and the FOOL, no one stands without permission until the CHIEF goes off.

Later, JAKADIYA enters and goes down on her right knee with head lowered to receive the CHIEF's instructions.

ARABS, entering SHEIKH MAS'UD's presence for the Muharram feast scene, bend from the waist to the SHEIKH, at the same time raising the four fingertips of the right hand together to the forehead briefly. The ARABS sit cross-legged with elbows on their knees when at rest.

RAUHANI moves always with dignified, medium-paced, floating steps with forearms parallel to the stage, palms downward, one hand over the other below the chin (see photographs).

The HYENA's initial approach is, of course, stealthy. It would be simpler, and somehow more credible, if the HYENA, though crouched, is mostly on two legs, since it will be accepted that a human performer is playing the part.

The RAUHANI *versus* HYENA scene is a dance with the major part of the movement belonging to the HYENA who (like everybody else on stage) cannot see the invisible RAUHANI. It is therefore puzzled by the force which is turning it away from the boy, UMAR, and eventually towards the kidnapper. The guideline given to the choreographer in this instance was, in essence: 'startled movement at a tangent to RAUHANI's sharp hand gestures of direction, with sudden stops showing the HYENA's confusion, all leading to attack on the sleeping kidnapper'.

Unlike the HYENA movement on two legs, it seems more appropriate for the LIONESS and CUB to be on hands and knees while on stage—the movement being as feline as possible, with much use of the shoulders. Whenever the LIONESS has to leave the stage at the end of a segment of the Dream, the style of movement can be sustained, bent over, but on two legs for a swifter exit/entrance.

If a real camel is not used, the feature of a camel's walk which might make a human performer credible is the very dignified bobbing movement of the head on a flexible neck, stemming from a bent-over, forward-backward movement of the torso. Unevenly done, this can be hilarious and so might damage the mood of the scene. The original production therefore used a real camel (thereby risking a criticism on consistency: 'If the hyena, lioness and cub are not real, why a real camel?' It could be too funny—or too dangerous, is the unsatisfactory answer).

However, our second attempt might favour a human performer,* suitably costumed and masked.

The 'sand-dancing' movement for the sandstorm is as described in the text. The movement of dispersion of the caravaneers by the high wind is predominantly a seemingly uncontrollable backward stagger with arms flung wide overhead until all are out of sight.

Dance movements during the wedding scene are mostly by the MAWAKI (lead singer). Throughout his performance the women attempt and fail to get FATIMAH, the bride, to dance. This is traditional. The MAWAKI then does a comic turn, such as removing his top garment and tying it about himself in woman's fashion. So dressed, he can approach FATIMAH in a last extravagant attempt to get her to dance. A gift of a new *riga* is then proffered to the MAWAKI (by BUHARI, the equivalent of the best man). When it is donned, the donor joins him in a duet while the women are dancing in a circle around FATIMAH to much rhythmic clapping by all until the cross-fade of lights back to the STORYTELLER.

The first pagan dance movement before MAKAU's night raid can be a slow intense shuffle in two lines with performers' eyes downcast, led by one of them into a circle, while chanting. The ritual can be as simple as this or more elaborate. The daytime raid led by KWATAU interrupts a simple flute-accompanied movement by the hoe-held farmers, bent over in their rows and hopping backwards rhythmically after every strike at the earth. Real hoes should be used since they are important to the following scene of the attack on KWATAU and then on SHAIHU UMAR himself.

The musicians who entertain the CHIEF OF KAGARA in the court

* This decision is not unconnected with the unrehearsed scene of one of the directors being chased around the periphery of the stage by the chosen camel some three hours before it was due to perform.

are dancing while playing their instruments. Each dances in turn toward the CHIEF, bows without pause in playing, then moves to one side. The FOOL can add a hopping dance every now and then.

The game of UMAR's male playmates which is interrupted by the kidnapper, SARKIN ZAGI, is played by holding hands to form a ring of all players except one who will duck under the joined hands in and out of the circle. A call-and-response chant is repeated (see Songs). When the chant comes to an end, the loose player changes places with the ring-member nearest him at the time. The latter becomes the loose in-and-out player. It is when UMAR (learning the game) bursts too far out of the ring and over-shoots the re-entry that the kidnapper pounces.

The girls' game with stones, to one side, is similar to the popular children's game of jacks.

A mime can be performed while SHAIHU and the ARAB MERCHANT describe the Sahara crossing preceding the oasis scene.

Music

Music was sometimes employed for heightened theatrical effect to accompany movement as distinct from accompaniment to traditional dances and songs. The player of the *kukuma* was assigned to any independent movement of the RAUHANI. For example, RAUHANI leaves the STORYTELLER at the top of the alcove and moves down to circle FATIMAH and enter the lower rear section shortly after the birth of baby UMAR, thereby fulfilling his parents' request for Allah's compassion. This movement is accompanied, not only by sound effects of wind and thunder, with lightning effects interspersed, but also by the *kukuma*, a relatively high-pitched one-stringed instrument played with a bow.

The *goge* is a relatively low-pitched one-stringed instrument also played with a bow. This was used to accompany movement of the HYENA and then for the LIONESS during UMAR's Dream. When the RAUHANI confronts the HYENA, both the *kukuma* and the *goge* are heard in conflict with each other. For the production, the *kukuma* was tuned slightly higher than normal and the *goge* slightly lower for more contrast in pitch.

Both instruments were played on their own merits as part of the entertainment commanded by the CHIEF of Kagara after hearing the reports of the first successful pagan night raid. The DRUMMERS who accompany the SINGER provide background rhythm.

The *amada* wedding music is a rhythm played by women on large overturned halves of calabashes (average 24″ (60cm) in diameter) with short sticks. This rhythm can be made to blend with the *'yan kama* music selected for the singing by the men who are segregated from the women according to tradition. The *'yan kama* musicians all carry small drums slung under their armpits. Invariably, the leader calls a line which is answered in chorus by the others and some male guests. All is punctuated by the vibrating high-pitched cry with the nose held that is the height of enjoyment, mainly from the women.

Songs

The children's songs go like this in Hausa and an English version:

I (with answer '*Iya*'):

Kangal Kangal
Kangal Kangal (the name of a horse)
Dokin zage
Horse for touring
Ba shi ruwa
Give him water
Ka ga gudu
See him running
Kaman na me
How does it go
Kaman na ingorman doki
It goes like a good racehorse
Dokin nake ƙuru ne ba ka ba shi ruwa da ciyawa ba
It will not be that good a horse if you don't give it water and good grass.

II (with answer 'Kulli'):

Kulli Kucciya
Kulli Kucciya (an imaginary creature)
Kan ta ɓata gida
When he missed his own house
Ta sha duka

Got a beating
Had da mangari
A good backhand slap
Had da tsunguli
Also a shoving
Had da tokari
Plus an elbowing

From the inception, the structure and placement of the singing (except for that of the children's songs and the pagan song) were such that all could be done by one group, the lead singer of which would be expected to take other parts such as the first BEGGAR, ISA the praise-singing messenger of MAKAU and the Fatika NEWS-CARRIER.

We were fortunate to obtain *'dan kama* Malam Audu Muhammadu Ashana and his *'yan kama*. I am told that a good *'dan gambara* might have done it. Without access to these types of Hausa singer/drummers, the requirements might be fulfilled according to the explanations given to Malam Ashana which he then translated into musical performance:

1. The first BEGGAR must keep up a line of mendicant chatter while running back and forth with his bowl, offering it to the passing market folk
2. When the MAWAKI and his MUSICIANS enter into the wedding scene, they should do so with a song which continues while all the guests gather onto the stage. The MOTHER-IN-LAW calls a halt to this (not in the text). The MAWAKI then sings a praise-song for MAKAU and FATIMAH which must be lively and funny. This continues throughout the comic manoeuvres described above under Movement.
3. A song to start the entertainment called for by the CHIEF OF KAGARA.
4. The messenger ISA's mission is to get MAKAU's requests granted with obsequious praise, some wit and (even if somewhat forced) humility, in spite of the prevailing influence of MAKAU's powerful enemies in the court. This scene was largely improvised until set.
5. In Fatika, the NEWS-CARRIER must give an item of information

about the general political situation and then the news about the release of FATIMAH's father. All this should be learnt rather than improvised. The whole attitude is mercenary as assisted by the stage directions concerning passing gifts of coins.

6. A BEGGAR sings praises of ABDULKARIM upon the latter's first entrance. He earns a coin.
7. In the oasis, a desert MAWAKI and his DRUMMERS weave through the vendors and buyers ridiculing the tight-fisted and praising the generous. The songs would be relevant to the goods.
8. In Tripoli, the SINGER should enter with a catchy street-musician's tune which would easily merit thrown coins. This is interrupted for ABDULKARIM's direction-seeking dialogue with him. He then pretends, comically and elaborately, to be indignant that such a well-known compound as AHMAD's is being sought until he discloses that ABDULKARIM is already at its entrance. He resumes singing as ABDULKARIM, giving him a coin, turns to call for attention.
9. The first BEGGAR returns to KWATAU's courtyard to trade praises of SHAIHU UMAR with the FOOL at the end of the play. This was also improvised until set.

As it happened, the Tripoli song became the post-curtain-call choice of the performers, sung by everyone for the departing audience. This was simply one phrase 'mas al-lah' sung four times by the leader and repeated by his chorus:

The above is in the key of C, but the performance was in the key of F sharp.

These notes have included information gathered from Umaru Ladan (co-author/director), the late Sarki Aminu (then Director of the Maitama Sule Dramatic Group), David Heathcote (Costume Designer), Dany Lyndersay (Costumer), Malam Audu Muhammadu

Ashana (Musician/Singer), Tony King (Musicologist) and other members of the cast and staff of the first production. I am very grateful to all of them for their help and advice.

Ibadan, May 1975 DEXTER LYNDERSAY

Shaihu Umar

ACT ONE

[It is dawn in Kagara, near Bida in the north of Nigeria. The voice of the LADAN *(or Muezzin) is heard calling Muslims to early morning prayer. The empty scene is lit gradually by the rising sun as the voice of the* IMAM *is heard leading the prayers. Men answer. Soon there is the final 'Assalaam Alaikum' which is followed by the noise of people entering on their way to the market carrying goods and articles for their day's trading. Up onto the raised area, a* BEGGAR, *whose agility and strength of voice do not justify his profession, thrusts his alms calabash in and out amongst the chattering traders as they pass across the downstage space.]*

BEGGAR: It is you, O great friend of Muslims, who we all wish to behold! Here is Audu's son—a balm to all the sons of Adam! Alms please for Allah's sake!

[He repeats this and other pleadings and praises while, behind him, some SCHOLARS *carrying slates appear with the* IMAM *for their day's lessons. Some passers-by greet the* BEGGAR, *some push away his bowl and some give alms. When the last has disappeared, he stops to count his gains. The murmur of the* SCHOLARS *startle him and he makes off quickly. The* SCHOLARS *settle down with the* IMAM *and read from their slates, but they quickly take advantage of his sleepy nodding to discuss world affairs.]*

SCHOLAR 1: I have heard that some Europeans have again entered Bida. Could this be true?

SCHOLAR 2: I have heard it is. They say the *bature* came along the river—along the Tsadda.

SCHOLAR 3: They have now covered everywhere like *Yajuju* and *Majuju*. An Arab I met in Zango said that Egypt is now under their control.

SCHOLAR 4: Not Egypt alone, even all of Hind.

SCHOLAR 5: Yesterday a pilgrim from Mali was saying that a great Wangara warrior called Samure is resisting the French.

SCHOLAR 6: May Allah make him successful.

ALL: Amin!

SCHOLAR 7: Even now the Sultan of Istanbul is forced to consider these Europeans, otherwise . . .

SCHOLAR 8: What?

SCHOLAR 7: Well, as the saying goes, 'the white man shows his true colour only when he is finally leaving'.

[*They all burst into laughter. The* IMAM *is awakened.*]

IMAM: What? Go on, read!

[*They bend over their slates and murmur loudly for as long as it takes the* IMAM *to nod again. The two* SENIOR SCHOLARS *enter and stand listening.*]

SCHOLAR 1: May Allah protect us from the evil of these white people. And I have heard that the Turks are as bad as the *bature.*

SCHOLAR 7: It could not be.

SCHOLAR 4: It is true. How is it that you have not heard? It was Muhammadu Ahmad who drove away the Turks of Egypt from both Dar Fur and Sannar!

SCHOLAR 7: Ah! Is that the man who claims to be the Mahdi? Allah knows how many followers he has gathered.

SENIOR SCHOLAR 1: But is he the true Mahdi?

SENIOR SCHOLAR 2: It is almost eighty years now since Shaihu Usman Dan Fodio talked about the coming of the Mahdi. And now many people have gone to the East just to see this Muhammadu Ahmad.

SCHOLAR 5: I heard a courtier saying that the Sultan has received some letters from the Shaihu Bukar of Borno concerning the recognition of Muhammadu Ahmad as the true Mahdi.

SCHOLAR 3: There are rumours that Shaihu Bukar has refused to accept this Mahdi.

SCHOLAR 1: Well, Allah knows all.

[SHAIHU UMAR *enters, stops out of sight and listens. A white-robed figure, the* RAUHANI, *enters with him.*]

SENIOR SCHOLAR 2: Yes, but it is just such rumours that will cause much hardship to pilgrims.

SCHOLAR 4: How?

SENIOR SCHOLAR 2: Now the pilgrims will have to go a longer way to avoid being caught and enslaved by the Tuareg and the Tibu.

SCHOLAR 4: I see.

SCHOLAR 1: I have heard it said that the people of the Sahara have very little respect for the Shari'a; to them Muslims and Pagans are all the same—all to be captured and put into the market for sale like locust bean-cake!

[*They laugh loudly again which wakes the* IMAM. SHAIHU UMAR *moves forward and the* IMAM'S *anger fades into gladness. The* SCHOLARS all rise.]

SHAIHU: The peace and blessing of Allah attend you.

IMAM: Amin. And the same attend you also, O Shaihu.

SHAIHU: Have you all slept well?

ALL: [*Kneeling*] Very well.

SHAIHU: No, no, stand up. Very good. Thanks be to Allah and our Prophet Muhammad, the peace and blessing of Allah be on him.

IMAM and ALL: Amin!

IMAM: Our very important visitor has come to speak to our most senior scholars, but before we leave, I must tell you of his fame. I called him a visitor, but of course he is not, for he was born in this town. Shaihu Umar has visited many countries of the Arab lands, but now that he is becoming older he has decided to come home to Kagara and teach. Now, O Shaihu, you can begin.

[*The* IMAM *and the* JUNIOR SCHOLARS *leave.* SHAIHU UMAR *is left with the two* SENIOR SCHOLARS *whom he leads up the steps to the highest level (the roof of the alcove). The* RAUHANI *has preceded them.*]

SENIOR SCHOLAR 2: May Allah increase your knowledge, O

Shaihu. Was your father a Shaihu before you? Do you have relatives in Kagara? Why have you come back to Kagara? But forgive me if my questions sound improper.

SHAIHU: [*Smiling at his eagerness*]
Extremely delighted am I with your questions. Excellent.
But why eat with such speed
And have the food tumble out again?
For indeed patience, in throwing them one by one,
Might gain better results.
Never mind. To your first question—
Whether my father was also a Shaihu—
I can say, no, he was not.
A poor man he was, and a servant of Allah,
Who knew nothing except the cutting and selling of firewood
And due to this poverty, an early marriage was impossible.
Even when Allah willed that he should be married
He became sick not long afterwards.
Nevertheless my mother conceived
And, instead of happiness attending this blessing,
The whole world became utterly dark for my father;
The child would inherit nothing but his poverty!
My mother's steadfastness prompted him always
To bless her, to pray, and to solicit Allah's compassion
To attend whoever was to be born.
Allah is great! Allah is merciful!
Continuously did my father pray
Until the hour that he died
One day before I was born.

[*The funeral procession bearing the* Makara *and led by the* IMAM, *passes below. A voice is heard expressing sympathy.*]

VOICE: So Allah has received Malam's soul? Well, may Allah grant him peace and forgiveness, and may his soul rest in peace. Nothing can be done except bear this patiently because death is the debt which we must all settle. The only thing we can do is to pray to Allah so that we all die in the Faith. May Allah protect the household he has left behind and give them the strength to bear this great loss.

Kidnapped in childhood by Sarkin Zagi, henchman of the wicked Kwatau, Umar is tied up and hidden in a hyena cave. But the Rauhani, his unseen protector, watches over him

Abdulkarim, the Arab trader, accepts the young Umar as a gift from the Hausa trader, Gumuzu

[*The last of the procession passes and* FATIMAH, *the mourning, pregnant widow, is discovered seated in front of the alcove with her* MOTHER-IN-LAW. FATIMAH *is crying silently while staring forward at nothing.*]

MOTHER-IN-LAW: I have asked the neighbours to wait outside so I could talk to you. [FATIMAH *does not speak.*] I am talking to you, Fatu. [FATIMAH *still stares.*] You must know, Fatu, that this is Allah's will. This loss is for both of us. But remember before he left us, he was—all the time—he was praying to Allah to protect you and yours from misfortune. Many times he prayed for Allah's compassion to protect whoever will be born. So. Be calm. And don't worry like this. Especially now that your time is near. [*There is no reply.*] Fatu! [FATIMAH *begins the groaned rhythm of labour.*] Fatu! Get up! Let us go inside! [*She helps* FATIMAH *into the alcove and out the back exit. Thunder and lightning begin.*]

SHAIHU: It was about twenty hours after
In the power of the Most Merciful, the Compassionate,
And to the accompaniment of much thunder and
lightning,
That my mother gave birth to me.
It was indeed an occasion;
My grandmother and my mother's friend
Rejoiced over my birth.

[AMINA *enters calling and meets the* MOTHER-IN-LAW *at the entrance to the alcove.*]

AMINA: Peace on you.
MOTHER-IN-LAW: Amin, and welcome.
AMINA: How are you, Grandmother?
MOTHER-IN-LAW: I am very well.
AMINA: And how is the day with you?
MOTHER-IN-LAW: Very well. . . .
AMINA: And tiredness. . . ?
MOTHER-IN-LAW: None at all.
AMINA: So Fatu has given birth? And you now have a new grandson?

MOTHER-IN-LAW: Yes, indeed. . . .

AMINA: Well, congratulations. Where are they?

MOTHER-IN-LAW: They are inside the room. [FATIMAH *enters. Thunder and lightning continues.*]

AMINA: Fatu! How are you, Fatu? Really, I am so happy I . . .

FATIMA: Oh, my God! For Allah's sake, stop! Your joy is misplaced. There is this child, born a day after his father's death. Since yesterday the sky has been spitting thunder and light. What can we say to this death and birth, with the heavens shaking as if it will fall? These signs must have some meaning. [*Kneels*] O my sisters, pray with me for Allah's compassion just as my husband did until his death. [*The other two kneel.*] Allah, look on us with mercy and let the blessing of those who have gone attend us.

[*She leans her head to the ground. Thunder and lightning increase as* RAUHANI *appears, hands up in prayer, circles* FATIMAH *and disappears into the alcove. Thunder and lightning stop. A baby's whimpering is heard. The* MOTHER-IN-LAW *slowly moves forward toward* FATIMAH. AMINA *turns to leave as darkness falls.*]

SHAIHU: Seven days after my birth
People were summoned to a ceremony
At which I was given a name.

SENIOR SCHOLAR 1: Do you think that Allah bestowed his Compassion for your protection? Would you say that His Blessing has been with you throughout your life . . . ?

SENIOR SCHOLAR 2: Did your mother depend solely on Allah's Blessing to protect you? My sister's husband died, but she has re-married!

SHAIHU: To God I cannot say.
Allah's Blessing always attends us.
But . . . special protection? Ah!
During a sandstorm in the Sahara
I . . . almost . . . saw a figure
I had never seen before
And then. . . . But . . . I was saying . . .
To my belief, my mother never again spoke
Of what my father had always prayed for.

Young as she still was
She never lacked suitors.
One day as they sat together
My grandmother asked her . . .

[FATIMAH *and her* MOTHER-IN-LAW are already seated *spinning cotton.*]

MOTHER-IN-LAW: Now who amongst your suitors do you find most . . . manly?

[FATIMAH *pretends indifference as she grinds out cotton seeds.*]

FATIMAH: Perhaps my father's namesake.

MOTHER-IN-LAW: Who! Isuhu?

FATIMAH: Yes . . . He . . .

MOTHER-IN-LAW: Isuhu? For Allah's sake, what would you do with a troublesome man who, like a Chief Butcher, is always in debt? Who, in this town, is he not owing money to? In spite of your husband's poverty Isuhu was yet owing him money. And now my son is dead, he will never think of paying. That . . .

FATIMAH: Perhaps he is seeking to repay . . .

MOTHER-IN-LAW: Hey, have mercy on yourself. . . . Well, what about Makau?

FATIMAH: I thought you were going to mention Audu. They say he has three wives now.

MOTHER-IN-LAW: Even though he has three wives, I tell you he is good for nothing! What will you ever do with that miser? Especially when there is Makau. . . .

FATIMAH: Or Habu, the potash-seller. You know that he has many horses, slaves, and his trade in potash.

MOTHER-IN-LAW: What will you do with a world-traveller, as though he has eaten the leg of a dog? And you, badly in need of someone who will look after this son of yours, a task which I am sure Makau will be able to do . . .

FATIMAH: Makau? Mhm! All I know is that he is very strong. But very quiet as he is, when will he ever have the courage to press his proposal?

MOTHER-IN-LAW: Makau doesn't have to shout or keep pressing

out his proposal. All he knows is how to concentrate on his job, a virtue which has merited him the Chief's favour. Even Kwatau, the Chief's younger brother, who I have heard is about to send his own representation to you [FATIMAH *makes a sour face*], has not gained so much of the Chief's favour. . . .

FATIMAH: How can that be so?

MOTHER-IN-LAW: Touching on this Makau, I swear to Allah, if I were so many years younger nothing would stop me from. . . .

FATIMAH: All right, all right. As he is the one I have always been thinking of—night and day—the marriage can now take place. . . .

MOTHER-IN-LAW: Ayyururi!!! [*She stands shakily and does a small dance.* FATIMAH *smiles.*] Oh, you. . . . So all this time you have been making me fall lower down into the well you have been digging and digging under my feet!! Ayyururi!!!

FATIMAH: Ah, what is all this rejoicing? I am really in for it. Even before the marriage has taken place. . . . [*She starts packing up the spinning materials.*]

MOTHER-IN-LAW: What more is there? I tell you . . . if Allah sees this marriage through, to God you will have nothing more to worry or fear. Ah . . . Ah . . .

SENIOR SCHOLAR 1: But why did she not choose Kwatau?

SENIOR SCHOLAR 2: He being the Chief's brother?

SHAIHU: You know the way of women.
Maybe she preferred a warrior
Rather than a power-seeking-the-throne.
All the same, it was not long after
The marriage between Makau and my mother took place
And some days were spent in rejoicing.

[GUESTS *gather for the continuing marriage ceremony--men to one side being entertained by the 'Yan Kama, the women to one side dancing to the beat of the Amada music. The rhythms come together happily and there is some teasing as the women try in vain to get* FATIMAH *into the dance. The lead* SINGER *makes a great comic effort to help and is rewarded with a new riga.*]

SHAIHU: No sooner had the bride been taken to her husband,

Than I, who was two years old at the time,
Was taken away by my grandmother
To stay and live with her.

SENIOR SCHOLAR 2: How many years did you spend with your grandmother?

SHAIHU: Three years. Longer would I have stayed with her,
But for the fact that she died suddenly.
Allah is great! And never would I forget her
For the goodness she always offered me.

SENIOR SCHOLAR 1: And from there, did you go back to your mother?

SHAIHU: Very quickly, without delay.

SENIOR SCHOLAR 1: Was Makau's strength used only for guarding the palace or . . .

SHAIHU: Ah, Makau was the chief warrior
The chief planner of every raid.
Everything was peace and quiet until,
Alas, one day. . . .

[WARRIORS *enter, each one putting on his battle armour. The* FOOL *jumps in amongst them and, dancing, mocks them.*]

FOOL: Burrrri! Today, the month of quiet has come to an end, now that the rabbit has bought a dog! I can smell those who will be enslaved by the pagans to help them do some expert digging of yams. You! They will let you keep your sword to plough the field. Haaa. Haaa!!

[*The* BODYGUARD *and the* SARKIN ZAGI *enter heralding the approach of the* CHIEF.]

COURTIERS: Mind the door; ride well; and sit well, son to the father of kings. [*The* BODYGUARD *and* SARKIN ZAGI *spread their rigas for a curtain as the* CHIEF *enters and sits. They reveal him. The* IMAM *also enters.*]

CHIEF: You well know that when the pestle is up, there is no rest until it has done some pounding. I do not wish to learn of any one of you becoming a slave of the pagans! And now . . .

know that whatever you capture in this coming raid, a quarter of it will be your share. The rest I will use to all our benefit in buying saddlery and clothes from Kano, and muskets from Bida!

COURTIERS: May Allah increase your faith! The Goodness, the thousand-times-successful!

KWATAU: Wayihu! I am the son to my father's house; younger brother to my sister! I am Kwatau, the Powerful, the Lion, and the single-boned Uncle's son! Drink water and return to horse! Only women stay at home, and children stay on their mothers' backs! The freedom of these pagans has today come to an end!

FOOL: Fat as you are you speak fatly! There is nothing to choose between the easily terrified and the terrifier!

KWATAU: Who says I am not I! Who is like me! Who can match my power! And who can topple more slaves than I?

CHIEF: [*Laughing*]. There is no doubt of your physical strength, Kwatau. It is greater than your wisdom. But you know very well that the pagans are used to our tactics. Therefore, we must revise our plans so that we shall get all the luck we want. And so, Makau, have any new strategies come to mind?

KWATAU: Alas, may Allah increase your luck. How do you expect a new bridegroom to think out plans and strategies? And will his knees not weaken in the battlefield?

[*The* COURTIERS, *including* MAKAU, *laugh.*]

MAKAU: All the same, my lord, we are used to raiding in the daytime when they are all at work on their farms.

COURTIERS: Very true! Indeed that has been the time!

MAKAU: But now they go to the farm fully prepared in case of danger. Furthermore, they are sharpening their farm tools to increase their cutting power against our swords.

CHIEF: Then what do we do?

MAKAU: The thing to do is to wait until night when they are doing one of their pagan rituals. During that time we can attack.

CHIEF: Very good thinking! Let us wait then until dusk. Yes, Kwatau the Strong, you see how great minds work? Well . . .

we must all bear this in mind, that war is an equivocator. The Imam?

COURTIERS: The Imam! Imam! [*The* IMAM *moves forward.*] Well done, Imam!

CHIEF: Pray, Imam, for our success. [*The* IMAM *prays.*]

ALL: Amin!

[*They disperse. There is the sound of a reed flute. The* PAGANS *dance out, singing. The* RAIDERS *come from three directions carrying lit torches. They chase and fight and capture. Before they move out of sight.* MAKAU *is seen centre facing a big and angry* PAGAN. MAKAU*'s sword has slipped from his hand and he is now wounded in the arm by the knife of the* PAGAN, *who takes advantage of* MAKAU*'s subsequent stumble to dash off.* MAKAU *retrieves his sword and, giving a terrible shout, runs off in pursuit.*]

SHAIHU: And that is what happened;
When the raiders attacked
These pagans poor—
Not evil, but untutored—
In the midst of their worship,
The unfortunate were caught,
Some lucky ones escaped
And the least favoured by their gods
Died in the fields.

[*The court* FOOL *is pacing and jumping about importantly as he awaits the return of the* RAIDERS. *The* BODYGUARD *and* SARKIN ZAGI *enter and repeat their screening of the entrance of the* CHIEF.]

COURTIERS: Ride well, descendant of the faithful. Walk well, giant Elephant! Lion!

[*The* FOOL *sees the* RAIDERS *approaching and beckons imperiously. The* RAIDERS *come in one by one; some with slaves, some empty-handed. The* FOOL *is happy, but greets each one with some deflating comment. He is especially scathing to* BUHARI *who has brought no slaves.* KWATAU *finally enters with three slaves.*]

CHIEF: Well done, Kwatau! You must have been a true terror to these pagans! But . . . but I do not see my brave Makau? Where is he?

BUHARI: As you already know, descendant of the father of kings, Makau has been very brave. But bad luck caused him to be badly injured in the arm. For this reason he has gone to his compound to have his wound bathed and bound. He does not wish to appear before you bleeding.

SARKIN ZAGI: Voice of the Lion, speak!

BODYGUARD: Take your time, the successful!

CHIEF: I understand. But how many slaves has he captured?

KWAṬAU: May Allah make you live long! Before you know how many slaves he captured I would like to open your eyes which I can see it is your will to keep closed about Makau. Who will not now reward you with the night after you have helped him get the sun? It is not without cause that you hear me denounce the man for whom you have such absolute trust.

SARKIN ZAGI: May Allah increase your reign, it was told to me that from the moment all the warriors departed for this raid, this man never stopped from condemning your reign. Shantali did not even know when Makau drew his sword to cut off his head. If it had not been for a friend the worst would have happened.

SHANTALI: Yes, O descendant of the faithful, and Makau did not go home because of the injury he received. He captured five slaves, but one died because of the great blow he received on the head. The four remaining . . .

CHIEF: I know my great Makau is capable of that! Ah, five slaves! So, before he comes let us hear some music to put us in the mood for rejoicing.

[*The* FOOL *claps his hands sharply and* MUSICIANS *and* DANCERS *take their turns to perform directly in front of the* CHIEF. *After some time of this,* MAKAU *comes in with two slaves.* There is sudden quiet. The* FOOL *dismisses the* ENTERTAINERS. MAKAU *prostrates himself before the* CHIEF.]

* If a two- or three-year-old actor can be found to come in with Makau and sit quietly throughout the scene that follows, he can do so followed by the Rauhani who would stand still nearby. The scene can proceed without them, however.

MAKAU: May Allah increase your faith. Please will you allow me to ask the entertainers to continue?

[*The* CHIEF*'s pleasure has turned into confusion.*]

CHIEF: Makau, so you're here?

MAKAU: But, your majesty, I had asked my friend Buhari to bring you an explanation. Or . . .

[BUHARI *makes a gesture to remind the* CHIEF *who brushes it aside.*]

CHIEF: Yes, I have heard! But how many slaves have you captured?

[MAKAU *is puzzled.*]

MAKAU: May Allah increase your wealth, these are the two slaves I have captured.

CHIEF: Is that so? You are sure it is two slaves you have brought home to Kagara?

MAKAU: May Allah increase your faith.

CHIEF: Do you agree that if I find some fault in your statement that anything can be done to you?

MAKAU: I agree.

CHIEF: Sarkin Zagi!

SARKIN ZAGI: May you live long.

CHIEF: How many slaves did Makau capture?

SARKIN ZAGI: Four slaves, may Allah increase your reign. But he entered this town with only two slaves, having sold the other two to a caravan of Kanawa who were going to Bauchi to buy locust-bean cake. Is that not so, hypocrite?

CHIEF: Is there anyone who will speak for Makau?

[BUHARI *moves as though to speak but is frightened by the look on* KWATAU*'s face and is quiet.*]

CHIEF: Well, Makau? What will you say?

MAKAU: Your majesty, it is only the elephant that can answer the call of the forest. As for me I have nothing to say since the pond has dried up and the forest is on fire.

CHIEF: You are rude! Quick now, go and loot his house!

SYMPATHETIC COURTIERS: Generosity, O Lion! He will be grateful!

MAKAU: May Allah increase your faith, look upon me with mercy. In my compound there is a mare and her foal, some goats and a few of the cows which are not mine. They belong to this boy whose mother I married. . . .

RIVAL COURTIERS: Mhm! Do you hear that! He has already started to lie!

SARKIN ZAGI: Where have you seen the property of an orphan to be in charge of it? This property he is spouting of, may Allah increase your success, is with the boy's mother, and she best knows where she keeps it. Indeed, who will ever make the mistake of trusting this man with his property!

CHIEF: Well, Makau, this is the result of your dishonesty! When I trusted you more than anyone in my court! I doubt whether anybody could have deceived me for so long without being discovered. I believe this dishonesty must be of recent birth in your brain. Greed is the key to hardship, and this is exactly what has happened to you. *Kash!* What I am going to do to you is much against my wish. Your house will not be looted, but from now I do not wish to see you any more! I banish you. Leave my land!

SYMPATHETIC COURTIERS: He is grateful!

CHIEF: Your family can follow you, but do not force them!

MAKAU: I have heard, Your Majesty, and I agree. But I am pleading from the shadow of your power, to grant me only two days so as to prepare for my long journey.

SARKIN ZAGI: This thief asks for too many favours like the son of musicians . . . tell us, man, are you related to any one of them? Eh?

CHIEF: Because of past good deeds of yours, I grant you the two days you ask. But now you have been in my eyes too long. Get out and leave me. Now! [KWATAU *orders the confiscation of* MAKAU*'s sword of office which he places on* SHANTALI. *The* CHIEF *is screened as he leaves in the midst of praises from his* COURTIERS. *The* FOOL *offers much comic contempt to* MAKAU*'s back as he moves out of sight.*]

FOOL: What happens when night comes while playing *dara!* Today the wall has fallen, what will happen now! What will happen now! Whoever wrestles with the tortoise and gets him on his back is really finished with him! [*The* FOOL *then realises that the palace is empty and he is alone.*] O, look at it! The market is over! [*He runs out in leaps and bounds.*]

SHAIHU: When Makau went home
He gathered his family
And told them all that had happened.
Three times he asked them
Whether they would follow him
And three times they answered yes.
My mother, from that moment,
Began to cry uncontrollably.

MAKAU: Fatsuma, this matter is beyond crying. Only Allah can crush the evil intentions of Man. It is Kwatau with the help of Sarkin Zagi who have planned this. Allah is most powerful. Listen to me. I will go alone, and then you can come to me later after I have found a good place. You must have absolute faith that Allah will take care of everything.

FATIMAH: I have no doubt that Allah will be merciful. But I am so confused. I was waiting for you to return home from this raid to ask your permission to visit my parents in Fatika. And now this darkness has come and closed around you . . .

MAKAU: I understand. The news about your father and his quarrel with his neighbours—this is very confusing. You must go and see your parents. But . . . listen to me: whenever you are going make sure you put the boy into the care of trusted friends. I will send a message to the Chief when I have worked . . .

[KWATAU *and* SARKIN ZAGI *enter brusquely. The latter shouts:*]

SARKIN ZAGI: Makau! Makau! [MAKAU*'s household runs out at the noise. The young* UMAR *is brought out and put in* FATIMAH*'s arms. They cry.*]

HOUSEHOLD: What is it? Fatsuma! What is happening . . . ?

SARKIN ZAGI: Be quick, Makau! And you silly people! With all this crying. Do you think we have come to a house of mourning? Allah! You must all be very stupid! Get from our sight!

[*The group runs back into the house.*]

Makau! Look how you have filled your house with thieves!

[MAKAU *moves briefly to* FATIMAH*'s side and touches* UMAR*'s face.*]

KWATAU: It is the Chief who has sent us to see you to the border of Zazzau. This will ensure that you have really gone. Whoever challenges us . . .
SARKIN ZAGI: Who would dare to do that?
MAKAU: I am now ready.

[*They push him round the back.*]

SHAIHU: And that is how those villains followed
My good step-father out of Kagara.
Allah is great! I remember when later
I searched and found Makau
Very old and almost losing
The use of all his senses
He still recalled the painful testimony
Of how Kwatau and Sarkin Zagi
Tortured and cursed him all the way.

[MAKAU *staggers in, pursued by* KWATAU *and* SARKIN ZAGI, *pushing.*]

KWATAU: Go on, you bastard! Now stop here! This is the border!
SARKIN ZAGI: Dishonest bastard! For such a long time you have been cheating the Follower of the Prophet, and Servant of God! This is now your reward! Hypocrite! Son of hypocrites! Come, to our horses.

[*They beat him up some more and leave him groaning. After a moment, a voice is heard, followed by the entrance of a* HUNTER.]

HUNTER: Nobody ventures into the forest unprepared unless the fellow is a fool or is mad. [*He stops as he sees* MAKAU *on the ground.*] Ah brother! Why are you sleeping in the middle of the road? Are you not afraid to be trampled by passing horses? Ah, wake up and move to one side. Assha! Are you hurt? Come, try to get up. Now! Yes. Again! Yes. Ah, are you up now? No! Hold up! Yes. Over to this rock. Yes. So. Yes. Ah. Here, take some water. Yes, that's it. Not too much! I have a long journey still. Yes.

[*They are seated at the front of the main raised area.*]

MAKAU: Thank you. May Allah reward you.
HUNTER: You look so bloody as though some horses have already trampled on you.
MAKAU: To Allah, it was two donkeys.
HUNTER: Donkeys?
MAKAU: Yes, in human form. One of them was Kwatau who has in his power the other, that is, Sarkin Zagi . . . of the Chief of Kagara.
HUNTER: Kwatau! Yes, I have heard of this Kwatau, and none of what I heard is good. His evil heart has won him many enemies. [MAKAU *groans.*] Look, there is no sign that you will soon be well. Though I am not going to wait for you, there are some good people in Makarfi if you can get there.
MAKAU: Makarfi?
HUNTER: Yes. It is fifteen days' journey from here, if you take this way. But look, take with you this charm of invisibility. It will help you reach Makarfi safely.

[*The* HUNTER *places the charm in* MAKAU'*s hand and walks on briskly. As* MAKAU *turns the charm over in his palm, two* TRAVELLERS *come from the same direction as the hunter. They are talking while they walk. One of them unwraps a blanket which he shakes and spreads in the space at the foot of the rock where* MAKAU *would have been if he had not quickly jumped up onto the rock to be out of the way. He realises, as he looks at the charm, that the* TRAVELLERS *cannot see him. He then has various silent reactions to their conversation while they eat.*]

TRAVELLER I: That was a very profitable raid which our Chief ordered on the pagans. It is a pity Makau had to be banished because of Kwatau's jealousy.

TRAVELLER 2: Oh, I know Kwatau lied much, but you must agree that Makau was too much in the Chief's favour. Most of the warriors were jealous of him. You noticed no one spoke on his behalf?

TRAVELLER 1: The Chief was very angry.

TRAVELLER 2: He would have been more angry if he had heard what Kwatau did to my brother who was on the raid.

TRAVELLER 1: What was that?

TRAVELLER 2: Well, my brother had quarrelled with Kwatau last week, and Kwatau was angry and seeking revenge. My brother was sick and had captured only one seven-year-old boy in the raid. He stopped to rest when Kwatau rode up and told him that the boy was his since he had captured the father and that my brother had only managed to grab the son as he was running away. My brother denied this and accused Kwatau of trying to rob him. Kwatau then drew his sword and said to my brother, 'Damn you! This family belongs to me. And if you will not give up the boy, I will show you who holds him captive'. And without another word Kwatau swung his sword and cut off the boy's head. He then turned to my brother and said, 'You captured him, therefore you take the trunk and I will be satisfied with the head'.

TRAVELLER 1: What an evil seed there! Aah!

TRAVELLER 2: Very well! Now that Kwatau has got rid of Makau perhaps someone can get rid of him, so that we can all rest in peace.

[*They toss away the bones from their meal and prepare to leave. As they go* MAKAU *shakes a fist at them, then sees something on the ground. He takes up a bulging purse of money. Jumping for joy, despite his injuries, he starts off for Makarfi.*]

SHAIHU: Having found a purse of money
Makau then forgot the charm.
He said he should have kept it
To save him from his later misfortune.
But the charm he did not miss

Because his natural manner won him friends;
At the Gate to the City of Zazzau
The gatekeeper was charmed by Makau
Whom he fed and lodged and cared for
Until he was fit to travel to Makarfi.
Furthermore, Makau received a letter
To the gatekeeper's brother, Tanimu, in Makarfi
For help in sugar-cane farming, on land
Which they had jointly inherited.
As to the money Makau found,
He invested in land of his own
And soon he prospered
Enough to send for his family.
He chose a shrewd messenger, Isa,
Whom he sent to the Chief of Kagara.

[*The* COURTIERS *are assembled three years later in the* CHIEF'*s court. The voice of the* COURT FOOL *precedes his entrance.*]

FOOL: The wall of the world! The learned! Plant of the rock, you only come out when you are prepared! What a sight for your people!

BODYGUARD/SARKIN ZAGI: Up, Son of the father of Chiefs! Walk in peace, son of the Prophet's Follower! Sit well, the one-thousand-times-lucky!

[ISA *enters singing praises and punctuating them on a small drum held under his arm.*]

ISA: The one-thousand-times-lucky, be good always, O powerful lion! May Allah help the Chief, and the Chief help his subjects. . . .

SARKIN ZAGI: Eh! Eh! On your knees! [*To* CHIEF.] O fortunate one, do not yet speak!

ISA: Under the shadow of the Chief, in the Chief's wealth, in the . . .

SARKIN ZAGI: Speak up, for Allah's sake. Say what has brought you here. Who sent you?

ISA: My master is called Makau.

SARKIN ZAGI: Makau! That thief, and good-for-trouble renegade!

If he is the one who sent you, well may Allah damn both of you! [*To the* CHIEF.] We are awaiting you, son of the father of Chiefs.

ISA: I am only a messenger and I have been asked to deliver these gifts.

[*The* SARKIN ZAGI *takes the articles and examines them carefully*.]

SARKIN ZAGI: May Allah make you successful; this messenger has brought horse-trappings, a gown made of nupe cloth and a pair of slippers from Tunis. Shantali, take these to the stable. [SHANTALI *takes them and leaves*.]

ISA: Ayyururi!

SARKIN ZAGI: Allah! Do you think this is a wedding party? What name do they call you?

ISA: Isa...

SARKIN ZAGI: I have come across a good many Isas, but not an idiot of an Isa like you! Where do you do your singing?

ISA: In Makarfi....

SARKIN ZAGI: If that is how singers from Makarfi are, well Allah help you!

CHIEF: Isa!

COURTIERS: Isa! The Chief will hear your message!

ISA: May Allah increase your faith. As you have heard, I have been sent by my master Makau to come to you and ask for your mercy to allow his family to join him in Makarfi.

[KWATAU *gets up noisily*.]

KWATAU: Nonsense! This dishonest fellow has evidently succeeded in deceiving the poor people of Makarfi, and has prospered at their expense. These gifts he has sent; how many people of Makarfi must now starve because of his greed? May Allah increase your success, will you accept these... bribes...?

SARKIN ZAGI: Your brains are scattered, Kwatau! The Son of the Prophet's follower never takes bribes. Forgiveness, O lion, that must have been a foolish mistake of the tongue.

KWATAU: Well, are these gratifications going to be accepted so that Makau's household can go and join him in his new den of thieves?

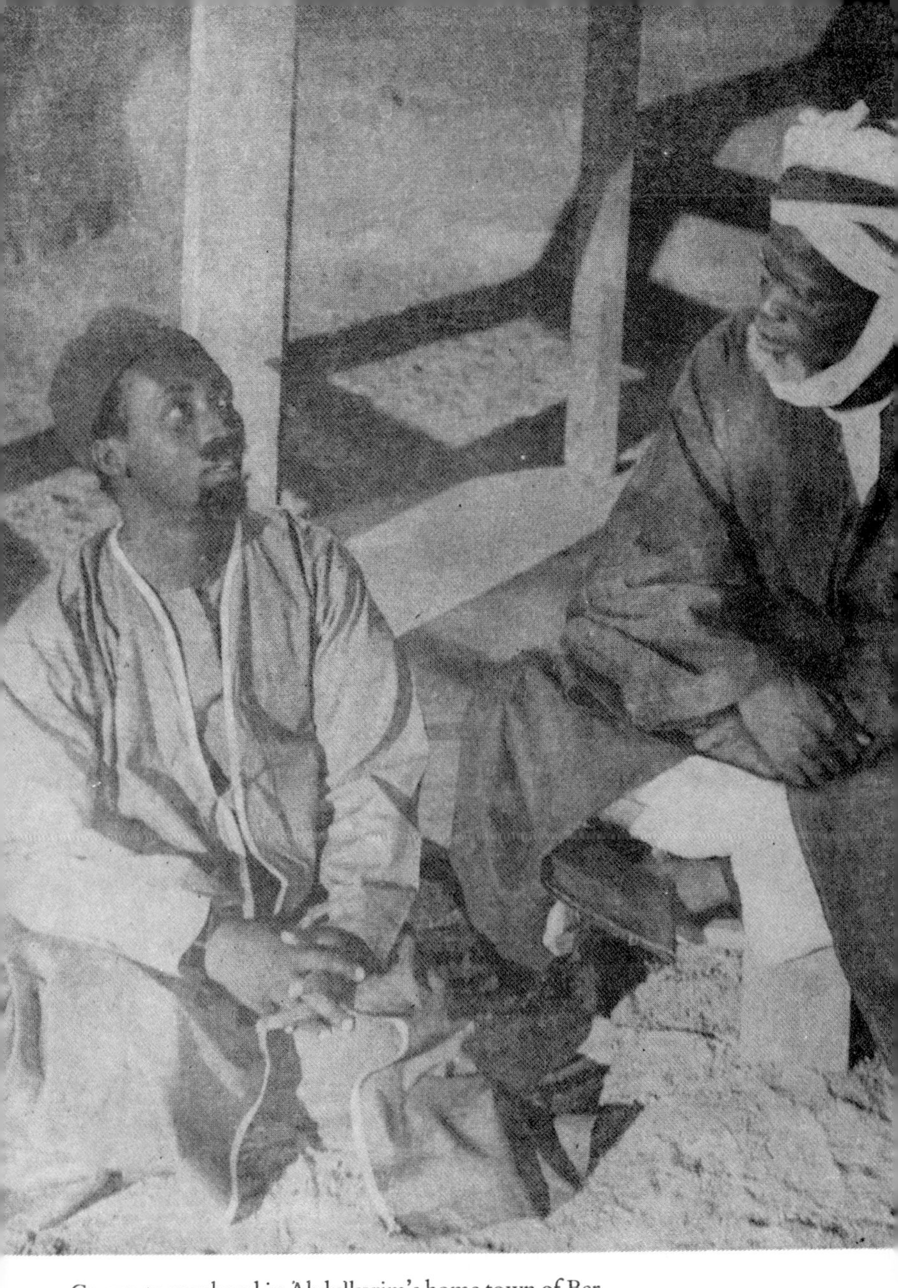

Grown to manhood in Abdulkarim's home town of Ber Kufa, Umar learns the Holy Koran from Sheikh Mas'ud

Kwatau, having succeeded his brother as Chief of Kagara, is a tyrant who brooks no resistance. Here he condemns the Court Fool to death for his insulting verse

CHIEF: What you say might be true, Kwatau. But remember; Makau was once my Chief Warrior and friend. I have come to believe through private representations from his friends, that if he did wrong at all, it was a lapse which the circumstances provoked. [*To* ISA.] Tell Makau that I have accepted his gifts in good faith and hereby give permission for his household to leave whenever they can. You may have two donkeys to carry the loads. Jakadiya!

COURTIERS: Jakadiya! Jakadiya!

[*The female messenger,* JAKADIYA, *runs in.*]

JAKADIYA: May you live long, your Highness.

CHIEF: Go with him to Makau's wife's compound.

ISA: We are grateful, and may Allah give you long life. I leave you in peace; and Makau shall not lose a word of all that was said.

[ISA *and* JAKADIYA *leave.* KWATAU *secretly sends* SARKIN ZAGI *after them as the* COURT *disperses.*

FATIMAH *and* AMINA *are listening to the* JAKADIYA. *Young* UMAR *and the* RAUHANI *are present.* ISA *waits outside the male-forbidden compound.* SARKIN ZAGI *hides and listens.*]

JAKADIYA: I have been asked by the Chief to bring the messenger your husband has sent. I think he has come to take you to Makarfi. And O! what a handsome messenger.

AMINA: Thanks be to Allah!

FATIMAH: Even though this is good news, my husband has permitted me to visit my parents in Fatika before joining him. I will go at once for I have heard that my father has been taken to court in Zazzau. But Amina, here is this boy whom I will leave in your care. We two are the same. Therefore consider him as your own son. Your husband will continue to teach him and I am sure he will benefit.

AMINA: I accept all that you have said. But Fatu, I am afraid of Kwatau. He is very much unlike his brother, the Chief, and commands so much power that he can crush anyone who angers him.

FATIMAH: That is true. First, Makau offended him by being in the Chief's favour, and even I earned his rebuke by not submitting to his lust. Let us talk to the messenger.

[*They walk to where* ISA *sits.* SARKIN ZAGI *is still hidden and listening.* FATIMAH *and* AMINA *greet* ISA.]

FATIMAH: To Allah, we are troubled by one who has evil intentions towards us. I have to go to my parents' town, Fatika, alone and I am leaving my son with my friend Amina and her husband who I am sure will look after him; but only if our enemies are kept away.

ISA: Yes, I know of your enemy. In the Chief's presence I have heard him with my ears denounce Makau in the strongest way. All the same I do not think—especially in a town where his good brother is Chief—that Kwatau will be able to harm your son.

AMINA: I agree. It is his brother's good nature that prevents much of Kwatau's evil doings.

FATIMAH: So be it. Here is this boy, Amina, and I hope you will be most careful. You know that the bad soup never ends in the pot.

AMINA: I will go to my husband now and tell him your warnings myself. I hope Allah will give us the power to earn this trust you have in us.

[SARKIN ZAGI *moves from this hiding place and goes around the back.* FATIMAH *goes into the house with* UMAR; AMINA *goes off alone. The* JAKADIYA *and* ISA *exit together.*]

SENIOR SCHOLAR 2: O Shaihu, why did your mother not send you with the messenger, Isa, straight to your step-father?

SENIOR SCHOLAR 1: Yes, it would seem that Makau's compound in Makarfi was the safest place for a small boy as you were then.

SHAIHU: I agree. But Isa was a stranger.
Amina and Malam Buhari were trusted friends.
I know my mother was concerned about me
But I was not worried about myself
Because I had many playmates;
Whenever I strayed away from home

Amina would find me in neighbours' compounds.
Malam Buhari taught me wisely in the mornings
And after his teaching period was over
I ran out to play with my friends.

[SARKIN ZAGI *returns to his hiding place with a shoulder bag as* UMAR *and his friends rush out of the alcove and start a circular game. The* RAUHANI *enters also and stands nearby. A small girl of the household comes out and moves to one side. She sits and plays a solitary game with small pebbles. The boys' game progresses until it is* UMAR*'s turn to run out of the ring. He runs too far and* SARKIN ZAGI *moves to him quickly.*]

SARKIN ZAGI: So all this time I have been looking for you, you have been here? [UMAR *stares.*] I have been looking for you to take you to your mother. [*He holds* UMAR *by the hand and takes meat and cakes from his bag.*] Here, eat these for the journey. Come.

[*They go off.* RAUHANI *follows. The children begin to cry, shouting 'Umar!' which brings* AMINA, *her husband* BUHARI *and neighbours running in to find out the cause.*]

CHILDREN: Umar has gone. Someone took him away. Where has he gone? Someone took him around there.

[*A flustered* BUHARI *is moving from child to child, but nevertheless takes charge.*]

BUHARI: All of you, get back into the house. I will find searchers to look for him. Allah is great! Allah is merciful!

[*The household enter the alcove and* BUHARI *exits with the neighbours.*]

SHAIHU: When Sarkin Zagi took me on his horse
We rode for many, many miles
And then we stopped near a cave.

[SARKIN ZAGI *begins to push* UMAR *into the alcove. He laughs. The* RAUHANI *steps into the alcove.*]

SARKIN ZAGI: You want a lot of meat eh! Let me tell you, you can have all the meat and cakes you want! [*He laughs again.*] Umar! Step-son of Makau, Chief Warrior of the Chief of Kagara. Do you know what will happen to you now? [UMAR *is about to speak.*] Tststs. Wait and I will tell you everything. [*He spreads a blanket for himself. Then ties* UMAR *hand and foot.*] Now. There is a caravan of slave merchants who will be delighted to have a small boy to do their bidding. [*He laughs evilly.*] This will surely earn me a lot of money, one thousand cowrie shells? Ten thousand. . . ? [*There is a shouting of 'Umaru' several times as from searchers.*] Eh? What is that? [UMAR *opens his mouth to gather breath but* SARKIN ZAGI *puts a large hand over it. As the* RAUHANI *begins to pray,* SARKIN ZAGI *draws a long knife which he places carefully at* UMAR*'s neck. The* SEARCHERS *enter and continue to call. The* RAUHANI *moves between them and the pair in the cave. The* SEARCHERS *pass on. The* RAUHANI *moves back and the* SARKIN ZAGI *relaxes.*]

Umaru, those foolish people are thieves looking for you to sell you to the slavers themselves. I know them very well. They are robbers of children all. I know them. They would not even spare me. Ah, let us now sleep. But make sure to wake me if you feel like pissing. [*He lies down.*] Ahh! To Allah, my hip! It feels as if it will break like a twig. Kwatau must change that horse. I cannot see how I will live long if I continue riding that horse. Mmm. Ahh. [SARKIN ZAGI *falls off to sleep. A* HYENA *appears, sniffs the air and pads slowly toward* UMAR. *The* RAUHANI *points sharply away. The* HYENA *tumbles. It senses the presence of the supernatural and is powerless to move in any other direction than that pointed by the* RAUHANI. *In this way, after a while of this strange dance, the* HYENA *finally is brought to where* SARKIN ZAGI *sleeps. The* RAUHANI *moves back to* UMAR. *The* HYENA *howls and pounces as* SARKIN ZAGI *wakes up and screams. The* HYENA *feeds. The* RAUHANI *moves over to the place where the* SEARCHERS *departed and begins to pray.*]

SHAIHU: When I saw the hyena rise up
And fall on Sarkin Zagi

I began to cry.
Some time later the searchers returned.

[*The* SEARCHERS *come back and chase away the* HYENA. *They and the* RAUHANI *follow the words with their actions.*]

They untied my aching hands and feet.
The news of my departure with a stranger
Had travelled as fast as Sarkin Zagi's horse
These searchers were too many miles from Kagara

[*All exeunt*]

They therefore took me to a nearby village
There they left me with a childless couple
And went seeking travellers to my town.
They found a Bida man—a trader
Who would travel in two months' time,
Meanwhile I spent my time on a farm
Working with my foster-parents.

[FOSTER-FATHER *enters hoeing in mime.* FOSTER-MOTHER *follows sowing seeds held by* UMAR. *The* RAUHANI *is near. The rest of the action follows the words.*]

There remained only a few days to my journey
When one day two horsemen appeared.

[*Enter* GUMUZU *and* HENCHMAN]

They came toward us with warm greetings.
They spoke with friendship but were evil inside.
We hardly had time to answer
When they had already captured us
And were pushing us to their horses.

[GUMUZU, *the* HENCHMAN, *the* FOSTER-PARENTS *and* UMAR *exeunt followed by the* RAUHANI.]

We did not know that they were raiders
Who captured their own people
And sold them to the Arab slavers.
They took us to the City of Kano
Where I became very sad and frightened
Because I knew that my mother in Fatika
Could never think I would be in Kano.
Even her friends, Amina and Malam Buhari in Kagara,
Had no idea of my unfortunate adventures.

[*In Fatika, a* NEWS-CARRIER *shouts the latest information.*]

NEWS-CARRIER: People of this Ward! The Chief greets you! People of this Ward! The Chief greets you! [*A passer-by drops a coin into his hand. He nods and pockets it.*] After a thousand greetings, he wants to inform you further about the news from the Sultan, concerning the coming of the Mahdi. The Chief wishes everybody to be calm about this course of events. [*Two women greet him as they pass and give him coins. He responds gallantly.*] After that, we have just received the good news from Zazzau that Malam Sambo Fatika has been freed of the charge of sorcery . . .

[FATIMAH *is passing by with a pot of water on her head. She takes it down.*]

FATIMAH: Wait, for Allah's sake, could you repeat what you just said.

NEWS-CARRIER: O! Malam Sambo Fatika—freed of the sorcery charges in Zazzau.

FATIMAH: This man is my father. How was he freed?

NEWS-CARRIER: The Chief declared that there is no such thing as sorcery in this world.

FATIMAH: The Chief said this himself?

NEWS-CARRIER: Yes . . . but only after he had been promised two milch-cows from two men your father had helped.

FATIMAH: Allah is the Saviour. But is there no news from Kagara?

NEWS-CARRIER: No. I have not heard anything from Kagara or Bida.

FATIMAH: [*Giving him a coin:*] May we live long. Here, take this to buy kolanuts.
NEWS-CARRIER: Thank you.

[BUHARI *and* AMINA *approach, hurrying.*]

The Chief greets you! Strangers to Fatika! The Chief greets you!

[FATIMAH *puts her hand up against the sun, the better to see the newcomers.* BUHARI *and* AMINA *brush past the* NEWS-CARRIER *and greet her.* AMINA *is crying.*]

AMINA: Fatu, it is us.
FATIMAH: Ah, welcome, welcome, but why are you crying, Amina? Have you been robbed on the way?
BUHARI: It is all very strange.
AMINA: We could not find Umar. [*She bursts into fresh crying.*]
FATIMAH: What . . . ?
BUHARI: All we know is that Umaru was playing with his friends. Then they said a man called to him and went off talking to him.
FATIMAH: Who was the man?
BUHARI: They said it was Sarkin Zagi.
FATIMAH: Kwatau's evil helper?
BUHARI: Yes. . . . But this is the strangest part of it. Some days passed and Sarkin Zagi had not returned to the palace. The entire palace, including the Chief and Kwatau, went out to search for him. It was out in a hyena cave that his body was found . . . half-eaten.
FATIMAH: And the boy. . . ?
AMINA: To Allah, there was no sign of him.
FATIMAH: And nobody saw or heard of him anywhere?
BUHARI: The news we have of him is not certain. I asked every caravan that came through Kagara if anyone had seen any young boy like Umaru. Three days ago a trader told me he saw a boy of Umaru's description in the compound of one Gumuzu, a slave trader. We came to tell you.
FATIMAH: A slave trader? Where?
BUHARI: In Kano . . .

FATIMAH: Kano. . . ?

BUHARI: There is more . . .

FATIMAH: What. . . ?

BUHARI: It was learned that Gumuzu was boasting that this boy, who we believe must be Umar, is of good character, and because of this, Gumuzu will offer him as a special gift to his best friend and customer, the famous Arab slave-trader, Abdulkarim.

FATIMAH: I will remember these names—Gumuzu and Abdulkarim. My father is safe. I will set out for Kano now.

AMINA: But Fatu, what of Makau?

BUHARI: It is true. He is there with his eyes open to welcome you.

FATIMAH: I will spend a night in Makarfi before I go to Kano. Maybe Makau can come with me. If my son is in Kano and will soon be taken to another world, then I must reach him quickly before they leave. I know my husband will tell me that Allah knows best, and that nothing moves but according to His will. I know this very well. If Makau cannot come with me, Allah will see that I reach my son safely.

[*The* LADAN *calls in the distance for the two o'clock afternoon prayer.* FATIMAH, AMINA *and* BUHARI *look up.* FATIMAH *raises her water pot to her head again as they move, talking, into the alcove.*]

END OF ACT ONE

ACT TWO

SENIOR SCHOLAR 2: Your life has been eventful, O Shaihu.
SENIOR SCHOLAR 1: And you have kept a faithful account of it.
SHAIHU: Indeed, I have spoken to many older folk
Who knew me as a child—
All in my search for the truth.
The truth as I knew it,
That is, while it happened to me,
Was hard enough to believe.
I found myself in the City of Kano
In the compound of Gumuzu, a slave trader.
This strange horseman had brought us there;
My foster-parents to be sold to his customers
And myself, because he was impressed,
He said, by my manner and behaviour—
Myself to be a gift to his favourite . . .
As a remembrance from him,
To the famous Arab slaver, Abdulkarim
. . . Abdulkarim . . .

[*While* SHAIHU *is speaking, a group of* GUMUZU'*s captives are crowded silently into the space off the main area. There is a burly* SLAVE-GUARD *with a whip and, immediately above on the edge of the raised area,* GUMUZU'*s* HENCHMAN *stands alert, his hand on his sword.* GUMUZU *himself is fussing over* UMAR'*s new Arab clothes. The* RAUHANI *stands silently near. As* SHAIHU *stops speaking, a Kano* BEGGAR *enters the compound singing praises to* ABDULKARIM.]

BEGGAR: Abdulkarim! Abdulkarim! [GUMUZU *impatiently sends* UMAR *into the alcove for his fez.*] People of the city and villages, the Emperor of Arabs with his caravans has come. Yes, no ordinary hand can hold fire: there must either be a blessing or witchcraft. [ABDULKARIM *enters.*] Whoever sees you has surely done his pilgrimage. The one who rains gold, diamonds, and rich clothes. The man among mere men who never falls. Yet he is the cloud above, heavy with rain, that waters the land. The true friend of the Arabs and of us all. [UMAR *returns with his fez on.* ABDULKARIM *tosses a coin to the* BEGGAR *who bows and runs off. The two slavers speak greetings in Arabic, a language which* UMAR *obviously does not understand as he looks from one to the other during the exchange.*]

ABDULKARIM: Salamu alaikum wa Rahmatullah wa barakatahu.

GUMUZU: Amin wa alaikumus—Salam, wa marhababika ya sayyid.

ABDULKARIM: Kaifal ahwal, wal hayawan?

GUMUZU: Ahlan wa sahlan ya sayyid.* [*He gestures toward the captives.*] These are only the best of the crowd. There are many others. Umar! Get some water for our thirsty guest!

[*As* GUMUZU *sends* UMAR *out of earshot, he explains to* ABDULKARIM *in mime that* UMAR *is a special gift to him. Meanwhile* UMAR *goes down to find that, among the slaves which have been gathered, his* FOSTER-PARENTS *are standing half-naked and with their hands tied. He is struck still, staring. He rushes toward them, only to be shoved away roughly by the* SLAVE-GUARD.]

GUMUZU: Umaru! Where is the water?

[UMAR *stands speechless, in tears.* GUMUZU *comes forward with* ABDULKARIM.]

ABDULKARIM: I appreciate your kind and thoughtful gift. The boy seems well-behaved, but I do not understand why he is crying.

GUMUZU: Ah . . . Ah . . . I assure you he has an excellent record, O great one. Ah . . . everyone likes him, and no one has ever complained of him. He is well-mannered and intelligent.

* ABDLUKARIM: Peace and blessings of Allah attend you.
GUMUZU: Amin, and may the same blessings be on you. Welcome O great master.
ABDULKARIM: How are you, your work and your beasts?
GUMUZU: Very well, O great master.

ABDULKARIM: I am satisfied with his excellence as you have reported it, but let me speak to him myself. [*He lifts* UMAR *onto the raised area and himself sits on the edge of it.*] You are called Umar? Well I would like it if you would go with me to my house in Ber Kufa. There you will be my son whom I have never fathered even with four wives. [UMAR *begins to shake, with his hands to his eyes.*] O! He cries more. Does he not like me?

[UMAR *wipes his tears and looks straight at* ABDULKARIM.]

UMAR: I do not know you well enough to dislike you, my Lord. I am your servant. But your country is very very far away. I can only be happy to go with you if you can promise to allow me to visit my own country sometimes.

ABDULKARIM: Ah. This is very simple. You can come with any one of my many caravans. In truth, whenever I will journey to Hausaland, I will ensure that we travel together.

UMAR: And again, O great one: my foster-parents are amongst the slaves to be sold to you. I would like you to look after them with great care.

[GUMUZU *makes outraged gestures behind* ABDULKARIM'S *back, but is all smiles when* ABDULKARIM *turns to him.*]

ABDULKARIM: This is very unusual, but I agree. I am pleased with the boy's sense of loyalty.

[*A horn is blown and a gong is heard signifying the departure of the caravan.*]

ARAB MERCHANT: The caravan is about to leave, O Abdulkarim, and we await only yourself.

GUMUZU: Umar! Run! Bring your bundle of clothes!

[UMAR *dashes into the alcove just before the slaves are driven by shout and whip across the main area to the exit.* GUMUZU *drags the two* FOSTER-PARENTS, *one after the other, from the passing herd to stand waiting for* UMAR. *As he comes out with his bag and takes his* FOSTER-MOTHER*'s hand,* GUMUZU *and* ABDULKARIM *make their final farewells.* ABDULKARIM *hastens out.* GUMUZU *watches in satisfaction as his* HENCHMAN *sharply motions the* FOSTER-PARENTS *out. As he is led away,* UMAR *casts an uncomprehending look back at them. The* RAUHANI *follows.*]

SENIOR SCHOLAR 2: You surely must have enjoyed the desert journey, O Shaihu.

SHAIHU: To some the desert is a romantic place.
True, there is beauty as you travel
But you cannot enjoy much beauty
When you are walking barefoot through hot sand.
You see nothing except naked backs
Of slaves sand-dancing in front of you.
Your eyes behold no landscape except red scars
Whips have made on those backs.

[*The* ARAB MERCHANT *has returned to one side of the raised area. The two do not look at each other.*]

ARAB MERCHANT: Greatest Mother Sahara!
You on whom man places his puny body
Struggling like an ant to reach his nest.
But puny man, dressed in arrogance
Challenges the might of Mother Sahara
And, despite the bones that mark his progress,
He ventures yet again upon the changing sand;
To resist, by his survival, fate's disinterest.

SHAIHU: On and on, in the bitter cold of night
And the blistering heat of day
Until day and night are one extreme experience
To which death would be a welcome end
Instead, there would be an oasis . . .

ARAB MERCHANT: The oasis is the breast of Mother Sahara
Put to the mouth of sucklings
Who traverse her endless body.
An oasis means relief from thirst

A rest for weary, travelled flesh
But also a rare opportunity
. . . for excitement . . . .

[*A hubbub of many voices rises as travellers are told by brightly dressed Arab vendors of the good bargains to be had from their heavy baskets hung on poles from the shoulders of pairs of slaves. There is much drumming in accompaniment to a singer who stops near each vendor to ridicule, praise (for reward) or try some garment or article in comic manner before passing on to the next. The* ARAB MERCHANT *and* ABDULKARIM *are seen among the crowd while the* FOSTER-PARENTS *and* UMAR—*the* RAUHANI *by his side—stare wide-eyed. The horn and gong once again signal the departure of the caravan and the* ARAB MERCHANT *helps to hasten the crowd off.*]

SHAIHU: We came at last to Ber Kufa in Egypt
Near the western bank of the great Nile.
I was welcomed into the household of Abdulkarim
Whose wife, Zainab, was happy at my presence.

SENIOR SCHOLAR I: Did she also speak Hausa?

SHAIHU: Yes, for she had visited Hausaland
By one caravan with Abdulkarim.
It was she who took me to Koranic School
I was taught by the old and wise Sheikh Mas'ud
Who was the Imam of Ber Kufa.

[SHEIKH MAS'UD *sits just inside the alcove, while* UMAR *sits at his feet in an attitude of prayer. The* RAUHANI *stands behind them. A voice (which can either be from off-stage or from* SHEIKH MAS'UD) *recites the first three verses of the opening chapter of the Koran—* Surat-Al-Fatihah—*in Arabic.* UMAR *repeats the verses falteringly. The voice chants the verses again.* UMAR *repeats them strongly. (Passage of time: either by lights or by* UMAR *moving to the other side of* SHEIKH MAS'UD.) *The voice begins the chant of the chapter of the Most High—the 87th—*Surat Al-A'la. UMAR *joins in confidently after the first few words.* SHEIKH MAS'UD *is nodding approval. The rest continues in mime while* SHAIHU *speaks.*]

SHAIHU: I learned chapters of the Holy Koran every day,

But soon I began to feel it was time
To go back to Hausaland in search of my mother.
This strong feeling had to be suppressed,
For the Mahdi's power had risen in the Sudan
And his ideas of religious reform had spread
In an effort to break away completely
By revolt from the government in Egypt
The routes over which I would travel
Were through a land in serious upheaval.
I forced myself to forget my mother and homeland
And continued my study of the Holy Koran.
On a Wednesday evening, in the power of the All-
    Knowing,
The ninth day of the month of Muharram,
I completed the long, joyous task set before me.

[*Two* SERVANTS *enter to spread a carpet on the floor in front of* SHEIKH MAS'UD *and* UMAR. ARAB SCHOLARS *and* ABDULKARIM *enter and sit lined on two edges of the carpet, on either side of the teacher and pupil.* SHAIHU *has continued.*]

Other scholars and Abdulkarim came for the ceremony.

[*When all are settled, the voice chants the final chapter*—Surat Al-Nas. UMAR *repeats the short chapter perfectly and with much feeling. Everyone is happy and* SHEIKH MAS'UD *leads them in prayer. The* SERVANTS *return to distribute alms and food and drink.* ABDULKARIM calls the BOOK CARRIER. ABDULKARIM *presents the books to* SHEIKH MAS'UD *as gifts for* UMAR.]

MAS'UD: These books of the religious sciences; prayers and remedies, are essential guides to the practising Muslim. Ah, there is Ahlari, Kurdabi and al'Ashmawi. My advice to you, Umar, is to begin with al'Ashmawi. And may Allah send his blessings on us all.

ALL: Amin. [*All exeunt except* UMAR *and* RAUHANI.]

SHAIHU: And, as Allah ordained, when Sheikh Mas'ud died,
God is Great, I succeeded him as Imam
And was there called Sheikh Umar.

All that was left to make me most happy,
Was to see and be with my mother once again.

[*The new* SHEIKH UMAR *is asleep on a mat near one set of stairs upon which the* RAUHANI *stands guard.*]

While the Mahdi's revolt swept the caravan routes,
I began to have nightmares strangely clear
Of which I could later recall everything.

[NOTE: SHAIHU'*s recounting of his dream will alternate with the real adventures of his mother in search of him. The Dream's mimed action will take place on that half of the large area at the back of which the younger* SHEIKH UMAR *lies asleep. The real action happens on the other half.* SHAIHU'*s narrative sometimes overlaps the Dream action. The alcove mostly serves the Reality sequences, but is used briefly in the beginning of the Dream as a cave.*]

Each night, for several months,
As I lay an hour or so asleep
I would dream of an old lioness
And her cub . . . at first, in a cave . . .

[DREAM: *The* CUB *is lying on its back on the cave floor, while the* LIONESS *paces between it and the opening.*]

Because hunters had captured and killed
The lion which had fathered the cub
The lioness has herself to go in search of food
Leaving the cub alone in the cave.

[*The* LIONESS *leaves the cave reluctantly. Exit, perhaps through the audience.*]

She has been gone for some time,
For food is scarce and she not skilful,
When two hunters come upon the cave.
They hear a faint sound within
And despite the hungry cub's feeble bite
They bundle him into a sack and depart.

[*The mime is as described by* SHAIHU.]

When the lioness returns without success
She scents the thieving human intruders
And, though sick with sadness and hunger,
She can do nothing but follow the spoor.

[*The* LIONESS *has returned, pawed at the place where her* CUB *had lain, scented the ground and now stands still, outside the cave, breathing with difficulty and growling softly.*]

Allah is great. This dream and its events
So much resembled those of real life
As reconstructed by me from later accounts,
That I was to dwell often on many similarities
Between animal and human life.
This is shown as well by an Arab poet:
'One and only God the benevolent—
He created man, animals all.
Created man the speaking creature;
Intelligence, wisdom, and sense of reason.
So made he the animal's mind—
Heat, cold, it feels them both
With Life and Death no less than man'.

[REALITY: *In Makarfi,* MAKAU, *now a farmer, and* FATIMAH *are sitting in his compound.*]

FATIMAH: Since Amina's husband has told me that the boy was seen in the compound of one Gumuzu, I would like to go quickly and find out.

MAKAU: Really, I am the one to go. But I cannot, because the sugar-cane is arrowing and needs to be harvested soon. My faithful Isa is away on an errand for seven days only. Wait until he returns and can go with you.

FATIMAH: Who knows what can happen in seven days? I think I should go now.

MAKAU: Well, of course you can go, and may Allah protect you. Here are some clothes that I have kept for you.

FATIMAH: Thank you, Malam. Until I come back then. [*Exit.*]

[DREAM: *The two* HUNTERS *have made a camp in the space of the raised area. The* CUB *is lying between them as they eat. The* LIONESS *moves toward them, but stops as a group of about nine* ARABS *approach the* HUNTERS.]

SHAIHU: In my dream, the lioness searches long
And soon finds the hunters' camp.
There she sees her cub sold to an Arab
She cannot know that this group of Arabs
Comes from two different caravans.
They will divide and go separate ways.

[*As the* LIONESS *watches, the* ARABS *have greeted the* HUNTERS, *bargained for the* CUB, *paid for it and departed with it, in mime as described.*]

[REALITY: *In Kano,* GUMUZU'*s* HENCHMAN (BA'IMANI) *takes up his position outside the alcove.* FATIMAH *enters from outside.*]

FATIMAH: I wish for you good health, but excuse me . . .
BA'IMANI: Your good health also. What is it?
FATIMAH: Please tell me: is this the house of Gumuzu?
BA'IMANI: Yes, this is Gumuzu's house.
FATIMAH: I would like to talk to him. It is urgent.
BA'IMANI: I will call him. Sit here and wait.
FATIMAH: Thank you. [*She sits on the edge of the alcove.* GUMUZU *comes out.* FATIMAH *stands.*]
GUMUZU: Is all well. . . ?
FATIMAH: Very well. Except I am asking whether among your slaves you have a young boy, my son, called Umar.
GUMUZU: O? Yes. But I have already given him to an Arab.
FATIMAH: Is this Arab called Abdulkarim?
GUMUZU: But yes, how did you know?
FATIMAH: Please tell me where this Arab lives.
GUMUZU: He lives in Ber Kūfa, far away in Egypt. [*He sees* ADO *passing by.*] Auha, Malam Ado! [ADO *moves towards them.*] This woman wants to go and find her son who is now in Ber

Kufa. Ah . . . the caravan you are in, is it going to Murzuk or Ber Kufa? [GUMUZU *has manoeuvred himself behind* FATIMAH *and gives* ADO *a signal over her head.*]

ADO: Allah willing, in a few days' time, I shall be in Ber Kufa.

GUMUZU: That is very fine. You can go with him, then.

FATIMAH: O, thank you. I am very grateful.

[FATIMAH *turns to leave. Unseen by her,* ADO *quickly delves into his riga and throws a grateful look and a bag of money over to* GUMUZU. *Then he follows* FATIMAH *off with courteous charm.* GUMUZU *and* BA'IMANI *go laughing into his house.*]

[DREAM: *The* LIONESS *moves to follow the* ARABS.]

SHAIHU: Because of the treeless sanded path,
She follows the two caravans by some distance
And when she reaches a place between the dunes
Where the two caravan tracks separate
She cannot see which way to go;
The heat and sand defeats the spoor
And, confused, she chooses the straighter road.

[*The* LIONESS *has mimed this action.*]

[REALITY: *In Murzuk, Libya,* FATIMAH *and* ADO *stop near a* CADI*'s court.*]

FATIMAH: Is this Ber Kufa?

ADO: Not at all. This is Murzuk.

FATIMAH: But. . . ?

ADO: Do not be surprised, woman. You are in Murzuk and you are my slave. I paid Gumuzu well for you.

FATIMAH: Your slave? This is not possible! I shall complain to the Cadi.

ADO: Do so. It is your right. In fact I was going to see him myself.

[*The* CADI*'s* HERALD *brings in a seat and places it on the edge of the alcove as the* CADI *enters and sits.* FATIMAH *and* ADO *sit before him.*]

FATIMAH: May Allah's blessings attend you O Cadi. In Kano, this man said he would take me to Ber Kufa to seek my son. He has now brought me to Murzuk and says that I am his slave.

CADI: Ah, I see. Perhaps I can help. But, woman, Ber Kufa is very far from here. Ah . . . well, I will see if there is a caravan going there. Bukar!

[*The* HERALD *comes in.* (FATIMAH'*s eyes are downcast in respect*). *The* CADI *whispers in his ear and passes him a bag of money. The* HERALD *moves to* ADO, *motions him aside and places the bag in his hand.* ADO *nods and exit. The* HERALD *dashes out and returns immediately with* AHMAD *who has given him another bag of money. While* AHMAD *waits, the new bag is passed surreptitiously to the* CADI.]

Ah. You are very lucky, woman, for there is a man going today to Ber Kufa where you say your son is. [*He claps his hands for* AHMAD *to come forward.*] He is here. Go with him.

FATIMAH: Thank you, O Cadi, May Allah keep you mighty.

[FATIMAH *and* AHMAD *exeunt. The* CADI *stands and draws out the bag of money greedily as the* HERALD *removes the seat.*]

[DREAM: *The group of* ARABS *which does not have the* CUB *has stopped to camp. They are armed. The* LIONESS *approaches cautiously.*]

SHAIHU: The lioness is confused and worried
That she has chosen the wrong path.
So, on the first night along the way
She creeps with caution to the Arab camp.
So disappointed not to see her cub,
So weak with hunger, she grows careless.

[*The* LIONESS *gives a low growl. One of the* ARABS *pulls out a pistol and shoots. The* LIONESS *leaps high and falls over.*]

She was wounded in the head and captured.

[*The* ARABS *go to the wounded* LIONESS *and lift her back to their camp.*]

[REALITY: *In Tripoli,* FATIMAH *and* AHMAD *are walking. They stop outside* AHMAD'*s house.*]

FATIMAH: Is this Ber Kufa?

AHMAD: Shut your mouth! What is this about Ber Kufa? We are now in Tripoli.

FATIMAH: Tripoli? But the Cadi of Murzuk said you would take me to Ber Kufa!

AHMAD: I know nothing of that! I know I bought you from the Cadi of Murzuk for five Maria Theresa silver dollars. And he knew I was going to Tripoli.

[FATIMAH *kneels.*]

FATIMAH: O Allah, protect me from these thieves—both high and low born. I cannot live much longer. O, where is my son. . . !

[AHMAD *drags her up and pushes her into the alcove.*]

[DREAM: *The worn-out* LIONESS *is tied on a leash.* ARABS *gather round, jeering and throwing pebbles.*]

SHAIHU: The lioness is taken with the caravan
Far away from where her cub had gone.
The Arabs have more than enough food
And decide to fatten her for the market.
But she will not eat and, wasting away,
She becomes an object of ridicule and spite.

[*Suddenly the* LIONESS *springs toward her tormentors and, at the end of her leash, roars as mightily as she can. The* ARABS *are startled and fall back. The* LIONESS *then gathers her strength and puts forth a reverberating wail.*]

[REALITY: *In semi-darkness at the front of the alcove,* FATIMAH *is seen in chains as she echoes despairingly the wail of the* LIONESS. *The two sounds mix with each other in frustration.*]

SENIOR SCHOLAR 2: But how is it, O Shaihu, that your dream reflected the difficulties which your mother experienced?

SENIOR SCHOLAR 1: The answer belongs in the science of dreams which should be studied more.

SHAIHU: The work of Allah is immeasurable;
With Him everything is simple.
This dream re-awakened in me an urge
To see my mother, which I could not deny.
I immediately sought out Abdulkarim.

[ABDULKARIM *and* SHEIKH UMAR *enter, followed by the* RAUHANI, *from outside.*]

ABDULKARIM: But, my son, the Sudan is still unsettled. The Mahdi is in control of the country and no caravans should try that journey.

SHAIHU UMAR: Is there not some other way, my good father, that I may go home to Hausaland in search of my mother?

ABDULKARIM: Well, there is only the caravan route from Tripoli.

SHAIHU UMAR: Tripoli? If we go down the Nile from Ber Kufa to Cairo and then to Alexandria on the coast we can easily reach Tripoli!

ABDULKARIM: I know. I have done it before. But it is a hard journey. [*Sighs*] But I see you will not rest until you go. And I will go with you. For you know that you are my only son and the joy of my life.

SHAIHU UMAR: Today in this whole world I know that I have no other father than you. You brought me up, and you established me among men. I shall be ever grateful to you. I am glad that you will accompany me to my homeland.

[*Exeunt through the alcove.*]

SHAIHU: I can remember that on the ninth of the month
In which the old people keep their fast
We completed our preparations for the journey.
We embarked and at last—Allah is Great!—
After several weeks of river, land and sea,
We were in Tripoli and hurrying to the market place.

[*As* ABDULKARIM *and* SHEIKH UMAR (*with the* RAUHANI) *enter from outside, a* SINGER *strolls by with his band of drummers.*]

ABDULKARIM: You there. I want to speak to you. [*The* SINGER *is up on the raised area in a flash, eager to help.*]
I am looking for a slaver in this town who trades in Hausaland.

SINGER: You will want Ahmad, O Great One.

ABDULKARIM: And where is the house of this Ahmad?

SINGER: The house of Ahmad? The house of the greatest trader in Tripoli? You do not know it? Ah, but it is a landmark to all who visit Tripoli. There, they say, is the house of Ahmad, the richest merchant in Tripoli. Of course, it is here.

[*He ceases his animated praises to bow low and point to the alcove.* ABDULKARIM *puts a coin in his hand and as the* SINGER *begins his song again, he calls into the alcove.*]

ABDULKARIM: Assalaam Alaikum! [*And then*] Assalaam Alaikum!

[*The* SINGER *is gone.* AHMAD *enters adjusting his djĕllaba.*]

AHMAD: Ah . . . Alaikumusalaam . . . Ah . . .

ABDULKARIM: I am sorry if I disturb your business. [AHMAD *gestures expansively that this is all right.*] My name is Abdulkarim and I have been told of your intimate knowledge of Hausaland. [AHMAD *is honoured.*] Of course! Your fame is everywhere heard; excellent soap that cleanses dirt, night rain that is felt everywhere in the world. Tell me of any man who surpasses you in the knowledge of the roads that lead to Hausaland, because, Allah willing and with your help, we two are journeying there without delay.

[AHMAD *is well pleased.*]

AHMAD: You have come to the right place, poet. No doubt you already know that the route from the east is closed because of the Mahdi's uprising. The west? It is too long a journey and there are many robbers. Therefore I advise you to follow the route which goes from Tripoli through Fezzan to Borno. Except . . .

ABDULKARIM: Why are you silent?

AHMAD: Even though I assure you of the safety of this route, all the same it has one bad mark against it. . . .

ABDULKARIM: Which is . . . ?

AHMAD: Which is very dangerous . . .

ABDULKARIM: Yes. . . ?

AHMAD: Desert sandstorms whose crests are higher than the waves of the sea; whose darkness is like the darkness of the grave, and whose destruction spreads like the fire in a cotton farm.

ABDULKARIM: Yes, your advice is valuable. And as Allah disposes everything we pray for His protection on the way. May Allah let us live until we have fulfilled our mission. . . . [*They turn to leave.*]

AHMAD: . . . And protect you from the evil eyes on the road. But . . . but I have a small wish, I do not know . . . ah . . .

ABDULKARIM: Please say it.

AHMAD: I have a slave woman from Hausa country. I bought her in Murzuk last year; but she is of thoroughly bad character.

ABDULKARIM: How is this?

AHMAD: It is just that since the day Allah put her into my hands she has not done one useful thing. She is growing thinner every day, always babbling about her country and family.

ABDULKARIM: Well, what do you have in mind?

AHMAD: Well! It is just that she is making my household miserable.

ABDULKARIM: So, what is to be done?

AHMAD: Perhaps you know best what to do; all I want is to get rid of her.

ABDULKARIM: Well, I do not know. Bring her here so I can see if she is fit to travel.

AHMAD: Eh, Zulaikha! Where is that woman?

[*In a short time,* FATIMAH *is pushed out by the harem maid. She is in chains, which* AHMAD *quickly removes and throws back at the maid.* FATIMAH*'s hair is grey and her cheeks are sunken. Her eyes are dull, hollow pits. She sits in tattered clothes where she has fallen.*]

ABDULKARIM: How are you?

FATIMAH: Thanks be to Allah. How long since I have heard a gentle voice in my own language.

ABDULKARIM: From what town do you come?

FATIMAH: I am a Fatika woman. I left my husband in a town called Makarfi.

ABDULKARIM: How is it that you have come here?

FATIMAH: I have been looking for my son and have fallen victim of evil men who value money more than human life.

ABDULKARIM: What do you want now?

FATIMAH: I want nothing more from this life than to succeed in finding my son. This is what keeps me from going mad.

ABDULKARIM: Tell me, woman: do you know the name of the town in which your son lives?

FATIMAH: Yes. I was told he was given to a man who lived in Ber Kufa.

ABDULKARIM: Ber Kufa! What was the name of his master?

FATIMAH: They said his name was Abdulkarim.

SHEIKH UMAR: Abdulk . . .

ABDULKARIM: What was the name of the boy?

FATIMAH: Umar. [SHEIKH UMAR *is stunned. He sinks to his knees and reaches out to her.*]

ABDULKARIM: Allah is great! Allah who disposes as he pleases! Be happy and grateful, woman. Allah has looked upon you. Today your suffering is over. The one you see before you is your son, Umar!

FATIMAH: Umaru? . . . Is it you? I . . .

ABDULKARIM: My name is Abdulkarim and this is your son, Sheikh Umar.

FATIMAH: Sheikh . . . ? [*As mother and son embrace each other,* ABDULKARIM *goes over to* AHMAD.]

ABDULKARIM: How much shall I give you to free her?

AHMAD: Give me anything you like. [ABDULKARIM *gives* AHMAD *a bag of money and all but pushes him back inside his house. He stands aside.*]

SHEIKH UMAR: My . . . mother. . . ?

FATIMAH: I am your mother who for many years has been seeking you. And at last Allah has brought us together.

SHEIKH UMAR: And to God, I have just been looking for you. This present journey . . . but, God permitting, I shall take you home to Hausaland with me and . . .

FATIMAH: Ah, my son! Do you not see what I am. . . ? I know I shall never return home . . . seeing you is enough. . . . As for you, may Allah take you home safely . . . to see the rest of your kinsmen . . . go to Makarfi and Fatika . . . ask my husband and my family to forgive me. . . .

SHEIKH UMAR: Do not talk like that! Allah will make everything simple.

FATIMAH: Yes, my son. But everything is already simple. May God bless you . . . and may you live the rest of your life in this world and after . . . peacefully. . . . Umaru! . . . There is no Lord but God. . . ! [*She dies in his arms.*]

ABDULKARIM *and* SHEIKH UMAR: From God we are, and to him do we all return.

[*Exeunt carrying* FATIMAH. *The* RAUHANI *follows.*]

SHAIHU: God who disposes as he pleases!
My mother had suffered much in her life;
Her years were mostly of suffering.
Her dream of finding me had come true
And, in truth, she was exhausted, burnt out.
The mighty energy that Allah kept within her
Was dispersed in relief and happiness.
Yes. She died there in my arms.

SENIOR SCHOLAR 1: Your mother was one of surpassing strength of character, O Shaihu.

SENIOR SCHOLAR 2: I understand how your great happiness at finding her changed quickly into much grief at her death.

SHAIHU: It was seven days after she was buried
When Abdulkarim and I set out by caravan.
In Hausaland was Makau, my step-father.
On my mother's behalf I would ask his forgiveness
Knowing full well what he would reply
And, in time, I would come to Kagara, my home.
For it is said: 'Whoever forsakes his home,
His home will forever forsake him.'
So Abdulkarim and I journeyed once more
To risk our lives on the great sea of desert—
Bound for Kano and then Makarfi
Where my mother had said Makau still lived.

[*In the lower space, a group of* CARAVANEERS *enter moving across in the 'sand-dance', a trudging, slipping, up-hill-on-the-flat movement.* ABDULKARIM *and* SHEIKH UMAR *move ahead of the* RAUHANI *and the others. At the rear of the column is a camel, loaded with their belongings.*]

We had progressed nearly half the way
When a great wind blew up against us
And in that wind a solid wall of sand.

[*There is the sound of a wind-storm. The light lessens and flickers. The* CARAVANEERS *throw up their arms in fear and stagger off in different directions. In a sort of calm centre,* SHEIKH UMAR *falls at the front of the raised area. The* RAUHANI *quickly but calmly moves to bend over him, arms spread in protection. Darkness falls.*]

We were blown to all points and saw nothing.
A blanket of darkness covered the sand.

[*Normal light returns. The* RAUHANI *uncovers* UMAR *and glides backward a few steps.* UMAR *slowly looks up and stands weakly. The camel has remained at the rear of the space.*]

When daylight returned, I was alone.
The others of the caravan could not be seen.
Of my beloved father, Abdulkarim,
I never saw anything evermore.

[*Suddenly* UMAR *seems to see something mirage-like in the direction of the* RAUHANI. *He rubs his eyes and moves tentatively toward it, parting the air with one hand. The* RAUHANI *moves fluidly backwards out of reach.* UMAR *shakes his head and puts his hands over his face. The* RAUHANI *moves to the standing camel and draws it forward. When* UMAR *looks around again, he sees the camel. He gives silent thanks to Allah and goes to take the camel's rope. He seems to follow it off. The* RAUHANI *watches* UMAR*'s exit, then returns to the roof of the alcove and stands behind the narrator,* SHAIHU.]

I had thought there was nothing more
That could grieve me in this world,

But in Makarfi I found Makau near death;
Aged and child-like he remained for some time
While Tanimu and myself tended his farms
And saw to the comfort of his household.
I was there when the Chief of Kagara died
And Kwatau appointed himself the new Chief.
I prayed that reason would come with responsibility.
Only last week, on Makau's death,
Was I able to come here to meet with Kwatau.
He has grown from evil to greater evil
And I will seek to speak with him in private
To turn back his disregard of Islam's teaching.
May God forgive him for what he has done.

[*While* KWATAU'*s court, including the* IMAM, *assembles and his own entrance is screened by the* BODYGUARD *and* SHANTALI, *the* FOOL *has gathered about him in the space on one corner (just outside the court) a group of* CITIZENS *to whom he is addressing a tirade against* KWATAU. *Inside the court, the old, fuming* KWATAU *and the quiet* COURTIERS *listen.*]

FOOL: This pagan who denies God and His Prophet
Has taken the path to the wrong destination.
A vast, black cloud now covers the world
And only self-rewarding apostasy and evil prevail.
May God deliver us onto the right road
Away from this great, unprofitable shackle!
As a trusted friend, the common man
Should be respected, never oppressed.

KWATAU: Eh! Bring me that bastard cockroach!

[*The* BODYGUARD *goes quickly to the* FOOL *and drags him to sit spraddle-legged before* KWATAU. SHANTALI *roughly dismisses the* FOOL'*s crowd.*]

Nh! Who wants to hear your preaching on God and a Prophet you yourself have never seen?!

FOOL: May you . . .

KWATAU: Shut your mouth! Do not let me hear your voice again!

FOOL: May God . . .

KWATAU: Shut your mouth, I say! Is this Fool also mad?! How dare you talk while I am talking? Hauni!

[*The* EXECUTIONER *enters with sword ready.*]

Bring me back his head. Now!

HAUNI: It is done, your Highness. [*The* EXECUTIONER *and the* FOOL *go out. At some silent urging from the nearest* COURTIERS, *the* IMAM *bows to* KWATAU *in excuse and hurries after the* EXECUTIONER *and* FOOL.]

KWATAU: Let us see his mouth open in treachery when his neck is feeding the Hauni's sword. [*He laughs while his* COURTIERS *look uncomfortable.*] Now, I have called you all here to tell you that we will go on a raid for those stupid farmers who are only fit for slavery. I assure you that whatever you capture will be all yours. For myself, old as I am, I will lead you and capture my own. Shantali!

[*As the* BODYGUARD *screens his exit with* SHANTALI, *the* IMAM *is seen climbing the stairs to the roof of the alcove. He speaks hurriedly into* SHAIHU'*s ear pointing towards the court. There the* COURTIERS *have delayed their departure to murmur among themselves on some matter of urgency.* SHAIHU *nods to the* IMAM *and, leaving the two* SENIOR SCHOLARS, *he follows the* IMAM *back down the stairs. The* RAUHANI *goes after them. The* COURTIERS *have come to a decision and exeunt. Down in the space to one side, some pagan* FARMERS *have entered and taken up hoeing positions in their rows. Another plays a flute for which the* FARMERS *supply the rhythm as they sing and work. The* RAIDERS *appear in one group.* KWATAU, *full of himself, moves forward with a great roar. The* FARMERS *cower in fear.* KWATAU *waves his arms for the others to attack but, instead, they march off in another direction.* SHANTALI *stays at* KWATAU'*s side but is roughed up by two of the* COURTIERS *and taken away. The* FARMERS *realise that* KWATAU *is left by himself. They retrieve their hoes and attack.* SHAIHU *has caught up and starts forward with the* IMAM *and the* RAUHANI, *but* KWATAU *is wounded and he rolls onto the raised area. A big angry* FARMER *rushes to the kill. He raises his hoe for the death blow, but* SHAIHU *interposes himself between the attacker and* KWATAU *as the* RAUHANI *moves to the centre in prayer. The* FARMER *drops his arm in surprise. He raises it again to deal with the intruder, but suddenly begins to scratch at the air with his hoe and move aimlessly away. The other* FARMERS *charge forward with their weapons only to suffer the same loss of interest and direction.* SHAIHU *lifts* KWATAU *and helps him into the alcove. The* RAUHANI *moves through the staring, staggering farmers and goes back up to the roof of the alcove as darkness falls. Immediately, voices of* CITIZENS *and* COURTIERS *are heard and presently a crowd is seen pressing round the space below loudly shouting their disapproval of* SHAIHU'S *mercy to* KWATAU.]

AD LIB: You should have let him be killed! He is not worthy of mercy! He is unmerciful! He is evil! Take him away! Close the City gates on him!

[SHAIHU *stands near to* KWATAU *who is sitting dazed on the* CHIEF'S *seat nursing the wound on his forehead. The* IMAM *is near.* SHAIHU *steps forward and raises a hand in peace. The crowd quietens in some respect.*]

SHAIHU: People and brothers in Islam, I beg you,
Consider the lessons taught you by your Imam
Of Allah's infinite wisdom and forgiveness
Matters are not as difficult as you imagine;
Difficulties pass as they come.
Who has ever seen a farm yield crops
Where it has been badly infested by weeds?
Indeed whoever cuts off his fingers
Simply because dirt touches them?
My good tiding for you is: Forgive each other
Because forgiveness is sweeter than honey
And full of blessings for giver and receiver.
Your brother Kwatau has sinned, there is no denying;
His sins are long and wide and deeply tainted.
But he was born to your ruling family.
And should he ask now for your forgiveness
I entreat you to give it freely, for Allah's sake.

[*A grumbling murmur begins, but* SHAIHU *cuts into it sharply.*]

And now to your constant raids on pagan farmers.

[*The crowd is stilled.*]

You know full well:
As God created you so He created them.
Your raiding is for worldly possessions
Not for the sake of God and his Prophet.
You also know that we all leave this world
As we came into it—indeed we are true brothers.
The late Chief, may Allah forgive him, was a man,
An able ruler, but a slaver of his brothers!
This evil was also in Kwatau's blood.
And whose blood among us is free of evil?
I will pray, and ask our Imam to pray for Kwatau
To keep him and ourselves on the path of Islam.

[SHAIHU, *the* IMAM *and the* RAUHANI (*above*) *raise hands in prayer. The crowd bows heads. At the end* KWATAU *raises his eyes and stands touching his forehead where he had been wounded. He drops to his knees.*]

KWATAU: Thanks be to Allah! May he forgive us all our sins.
ALL: Amin!
KWATAU: I am healed. [*He is astonished for a moment, then stands.*] Hauni! [*The* EXECUTIONER *enters without his sword.*]
HAUNI: May you live long.
KWATAU: I hope you have not yet . . .
HAUNI: No, your Highness, the Imam. . . .

[KWATAU *sighs as* SHAIHU *leaves his side to ascend the stairs.*]

KWATAU: It is good. Bring the Fool here.
HAUNI: It is done, your Highness.

[KWATAU *slowly shakes his head as the* EXECUTIONER *goes out and quickly returns pushing the* FOOL, *still frightened.*]

KWATAU: You are free. With Shaihu Umar's help I will try to undo what I have done. [*The* FOOL *is startled, then joyous, then thankful. The first* BEGGAR *is in the crowd. He steps onto the raised area.*]

BEGGAR: May God look-upon you, O Shaihu . . .

FOOL: And on your intentions, wise and good.

BEGGAR: Ray of light, destroyer of darkness!

FOOL: Moon that illuminates!

BEGGAR: People of your stature are hard to find.

FOOL: Cool light of dawn that wakens the world.

[SHAIHU *has reached his former seat on the roof of the alcove and raises a hand to deter the praise-sayers. He first speaks to the two* SENIOR SCHOLARS.]

SHAIHU: Tomorrow, God willing, we shall begin our lessons. [*To all:*] Please join me in the closing prayer of my teaching. [*He prays, then raises his hands. The* RAUHANI *does the same.*]

ALL: Amin!

CURTAIN